3

SECOND EDITION

STEP FORWARD

STANDARDS-BASED LANGUAGE LEARNING FOR WORK AND ACADEMIC READINESS

SERIES DIRECTOR
Jayme Adelson-Goldstein

Workbook

Janet Podnecky

OXFORD
UNIVERSITY PRESS

OXFORD
UNIVERSITY PRESS

198 Madison Avenue
New York, NY 10016 USA

Great Clarendon Street, Oxford, OX2 6DP, United Kingdom

Oxford University Press is a department of the University of Oxford. It furthers the University's objective of excellence in research, scholarship, and education by publishing worldwide. Oxford is a registered trade mark of Oxford University Press in the UK and in certain other countries

First published in 2017
2021 2020
10 9 8 7 6

ISBN: 978 0 19 449337 6 (Workbook Level 3)

Printed in China

This book is printed on paper from certified and well-managed sources

ACKNOWLEDGMENTS

Illustrations by: Shawn Banner: 22, 46; John Batten: 37, 45, 71; Kathy Baxendale: 10, 19, 28, 59; Annie Bissett: 8, 11, 56, 63, 72, 84; Arlene Boehm: 9, 16, 64, 65; Kevin Brown/Top Dog Studios: 4, 19, 44, 50; Sam Collins: 51; Laurie A. Conley: 2, 15; Bill Dickson / Contact Jupiter: 9, 61; Jon Keegan: 53; Uldis Klavins: 58, 68.

The publishers would like to thank the following for their kind permission to reproduce photographs: Cover, Click Bestsellers/Shutterstock.com; pg. 7 wavebreakmedia/ Shutterstock; pg. 11 Dragon Images/Shutterstock, Ian Dagnall Commercial Collection/Alamy Stock Photo, RosaIreneBetancourt 9/Alamy Stock Photo, Panther Media GmbH/Alamy Stock Photo; pg. 25 Adam Gregor/Shutterstock; pg. 29 Pressmaster/Shutterstock; pg. 43 mayura benjarattanapakee/ Shutterstock; pg. 48 JGI/Jamie Grill/Blend Images/Getty Images; pg. 49 Hero Images Inc./Alamy Stock Photo; pg. 60 Zero Creatives/Getty Images; pg. 63 Minerva Studio/Shutterstock; pg. 72 antoniodiaz/Shutterstock.

CONTENTS

UNIT 1
Learning Together

LESSON 1 VOCABULARY

A Match the pictures with the words.

1

2

3
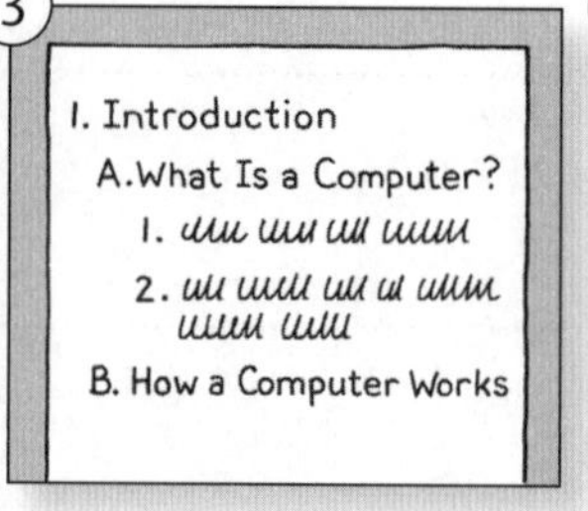

4

5
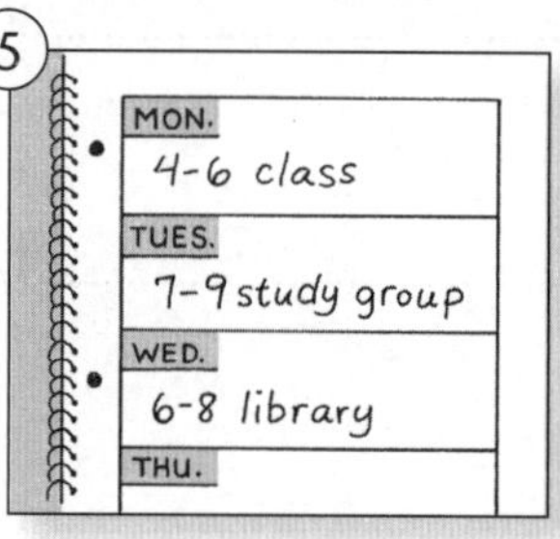

6

7

8

__1__ take notes

____ make a study schedule

____ organize materials

____ search online

____ make an outline

____ (do) research

____ take a break

____ memorize words

B Match the students with the schools.

__f__ 1. Ivan is 23 years old and studying for the GED.

____ 2. Sara is in sixth grade this year.

____ 3. Oscar just started eleventh grade.

____ 4. Carolina is in first grade.

____ 5. Trinh has his GED and just started a two-year program.

____ 6. Hetal began a four-year engineering program.

____ 7. Marcos is studying automotive repair.

a. community college
b. elementary school
c. university
d. middle school
e. vocational school
f. adult school
g. high school

A Complete Irina's journal entry. Use the words in the box.

to introduce	a presentation	first assignment	~~first day of~~
was nervous	to meet	talk about	about ourselves

Wednesday, September 12

Today was the ___first day of___ (1) English class. It was really fun. At the beginning of the class, our teacher, Ms. Hampton, asked us ______________ (2) ourselves. I ______________ (3), but it was interesting ______________ (4) my classmates.

Then we worked in groups. We had to ______________ (5) our goals for the class. For our ______________ (6), Ms. Hampton asked us to write ______________ (7). Then she asked us to give ______________ (8) about what we wrote. We all learned a lot about each other. I want to do another assignment like this again tomorrow.

B Mark the sentences *T* (true) or *F* (false).

__F__ 1. Today was the last day of English class.

____ 2. Ms. Hampton asked the class to introduce themselves.

____ 3. In class, Irina was nervous at first.

____ 4. The students didn't work in groups.

____ 5. Irina had to write about her class.

____ 6. Irina learned a lot in the class.

LESSON 3 GRAMMAR

A **Complete the sentences with the simple present, present continuous, simple past, or past continuous. Use the information in the chart.**

When?	Kate and Pilar	Marco	Marcella
last week	stay home	finish his class	write an essay
every day	listen to the radio	work	go to the gym
right now	study in the library	play basketball	read a book
yesterday at noon	eat lunch	drive to the bank	study for a test

1. Kate and Pilar stayed home last week.
2. Last week, Marco ______________________.
3. Yesterday at noon, Kate and Pilar ______________________.
4. Last week, Marcella ______________________.
5. Marco ______________________ every day.
6. Kate and Pilar ______________________ right now.
7. Yesterday at noon, Marco ______________________.
8. Marcella ______________________ right now.

B **Write sentences. Use the simple present, present continuous, simple past, or past continuous.**

1. I / not / study / right now
   I am not studying right now.
2. Alan / take notes / in class / last night
   ____
3. Hana / not / memorize / the new words / last week
   ____
4. We / search / the Internet / every day
   ____
5. They / not / take / notes / during class yesterday
   ____
6. Our teacher / help us / a lot / every week
   ____

C Match the questions with the answers.

__b__	1. Did Tim talk to you?	a. No, they don't.
____	2. Does he come to class every week?	b. Yes, he did.
____	3. Is he studying here now?	c. No, they weren't.
____	4. Are your friends in the library now?	d. Yes, he is.
____	5. Do they often go to the movies?	e. No, they aren't.
____	6. Were they watching a movie at 10 p.m.?	f. No, he doesn't.

D Read the letter. Then rewrite the letter with the correct verb forms.

Dear Sammy,

Hi! How are you? Everything is okay here. Yesterday, I study for two hours for my English test. I'm glad I did. The test was long, but I think I did well.

Right now, Barbara and Carol watch TV. They learned a lot by watching TV every day.

I liked to use the Internet to find interesting ways to help me study. In our last class, the teacher ask us to bring a newspaper article to the next class. Yesterday, I looks for an article about good study habits for a half hour.

Do you go home to visit your family last week? Do you have a good time? I hope so.

Talk to you soon,
Marcos

Dear Sammy,

Hi! How are you? Everything is okay here. Yesterday, I studied for two hours for my English test.

____

____

____

____

____

____

____

____

____

Talk to you soon,
Marcos

LESSON 4 EVERYDAY CONVERSATION

A Complete the conversation. Use the words in the box.

studying economics	should think about	do you like	~~thinking about~~
so many choices	not sure	worked in	hard to say

David: I'm thinking about a job in computer programming.

Luis: That sounds interesting.

David: What about you? What kind of career are you ___thinking about___ (1)?

Luis: There are ______________ (2). I'm just ______________ (3).

David: What kinds of things ______________ (4) to do?

Luis: It's ______________ (5). I ______________ (6) an office last year, and I enjoyed that. I'm ______________ (7) right now. I like my class.

David: You ______________ (8) a career in banking. It's a good field, and there are lots of opportunities.

B Read the sentences. Circle the correct words.

1. I don't always write (clear / (clearly)).
2. We are always (careful / carefully) and check our work.
3. In our group, we answered the questions (quick / quickly).
4. I think she teaches (good / well).
5. The assignment was (easy / easily).

C Complete the sentences. Use the words in the box.

well	clearly	quickly	good	clear	quick

1. A computer programmer must work ___quickly___ to fix mistakes in the code.
2. All of our study materials are ______________, so I can understand them easily.
3. I always organize my study materials ______________ so that I can find everything I need.
4. A teacher must always speak ______________ so the students understand.
5. An editor must be ______________ at finding errors in the text.
6. Some animals are ______________ and hard to catch.

DO THE MATH Go to page 86.

A **Read the website. What information about the library can you find?**

www.

Chester Library: It's for Everyone!

Location/Directions | Hours | Events | Questions

Classes

- **Intro. to Computers:** Mon., Wed. 6 p.m. to 8 p.m.
- **Learn a Language:** Tues., Thurs. 7 p.m. to 9 p.m.
  English, Spanish, Chinese: Beginning and Intermediate
  Spanish: Advanced
- **After-School Tutoring:** Mon.–Thurs. 3 p.m. to 5 p.m. (for ages 12 to 18)
- **Story Hour:** Tues. 10 a.m. to 11 a.m. (for ages 2 to 5)

Find Books and Do Research

Catalog Search
Magazines and Newspapers
Audio Books
Pictures, Photos, and Maps

Be a Volunteer

Library Volunteer: Help organize books
Story-Hour Aide
After-School Study Partner: Help a student understand assignments

We're Here to Help You

Get a Library Card
Sign Up for a Computer
Get Online Help

B **Complete the sentences. Circle *a* or *b*.**

1. _____ is a class for children.
   (a.) Story Hour
   b. Intro. to Computers

2. After-School Tutoring is for _____.
   a. children ages 2 to 5
   b. children ages 12 to 18

3. To look for a book on computer graphics, go to _____.
   a. Be a Volunteer
   b. Find Books and Do Research

4. To find out the library's hours, go to _____.
   a. Hours
   b. Location/Directions

5. Ana has some free time and likes to help others. She should go to _____.
   a. Be a Volunteer
   b. Find Books and Do Research

6. Carla needs a library card. She should go to _____.
   a. We're Here to Help You
   b. Find Books and Do Research

A **Read the learning survey. Then circle the verbs in the simple present, and underline the verbs in the simple past.**

ESL Student TODAY

How Do You Learn?

We asked 20 students about how they learn. Here's what they told us:

		Number who say yes	Number who say no
1.	I listen to the radio every day.	5	15
2.	I listened to the radio yesterday	8	12
3.	I use the Internet every day.	15	5
4.	I used the Internet yesterday.	16	4
5.	I speak clearly.	4	16
6.	I write carefully.	2	18
7.	I made a clear study schedule.	12	8
8.	I memorize words quickly.	10	10
9.	I went to the library last week.	14	6
10.	I studied English last year.	6	14

B **Look at the learning survey in A. Find three adverbs showing how they learn and write them.**

1. ________________ 2. ________________ 3. ________________

C **Write the correct percentages for the students who answered *yes*.**

1. 5 ÷ 20 = .25 or 25% of the students listen to the radio every day.
2. ____________________ of the students listened to the radio yesterday.
3. ____________________ of the students use the Internet every day.
4. ____________________ of the students used the Internet yesterday.
5. ____________________ of the students speak clearly.
6. ____________________ of the students write carefully.
7. ____________________ of the students made a clear study schedule.
8. ____________________ of the students memorize words quickly.
9. ____________________ of the students went to the library last week.
10. ____________________ of the students studied English last year.

UNIT
2 Ready for Fun

LESSON 1 VOCABULARY

A **Complete the sentences. Use the words in the box.**

farmers' market	~~amusement park~~	gym	zoo	nightclub	theater

What's Happening this Weekend at Fiesta Village

Fun for all! Over 25 rides for young and old! Lots to see and do at the amusement park. (1)

See all the animals up close at the ______________ (2)

Check out the fresh-picked fruit and vegetables at the ______________ (3)

Come exercise here at the ______________ (4)

Dance all night or just listen to the music at the ______________ (5)

This weekend is your last chance to see Victor Reyes in the play, *The King Enters*, at the ______________ (6)

B **Match the pictures with the sentences.**

e 1. It's loud in this place!

____ 2. I love this show! It's entertaining!

____ 3. It's very relaxing here.

____ 4. This is really boring!

____ 5. Wow! It's exciting!

____ 6. I can't move at all! It's crowded.

A **Look at the pictures. Complete the email. Use the words in the box.**

to a concert	at 5:00	Hi Oscar	~~Sunday evening~~
are you	get together	Think about	Talk to you soon

From: Petra
To: Oscar
Subject: Sunday evening (1)

________________ (2),

How ________________ (3)? I'm glad it's Friday. I'm ready to relax. What are your plans for Sunday? Would you like to ________________ (4)? Ali, Noura, and I are going to eat dinner at my house ________________ (5). Then we're going to go ________________ (6) at 7:00. Do you want to come with us? ________________ (7) it. I'll call you later.

________________ (8),

Petra

B **Read the sentences. Circle the correct words.**

1. Petra wrote an email to (Oscar / Ali).
2. The subject of the email is (dinner / Sunday evening).
3. They're going to eat at (5:00 / 7:00).
4. They're going to go to (a concert / Petra's house) at 7:00.
5. Petra is going to (call / see) Oscar later.

A **Look at the brochure. Write sentences with *be going to* and the words in parentheses.**

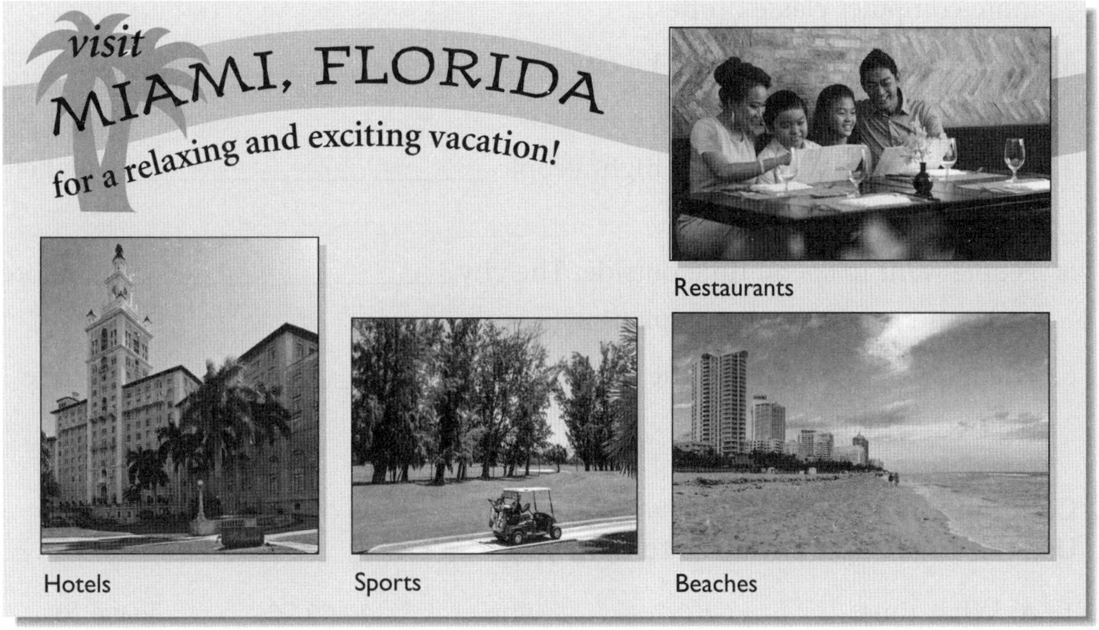

1. Ray and his family ___are going to stay in a hotel___ by the beach. (stay in a hotel)
2. His wife and children ______________________. (go to beach)
3. He ______________________. (play golf)
4. His children ______________________. (not sail)
5. His son ______________________. (swim in the ocean)
6. His daughter ______________________. (not swim in the ocean)

B **Complete the sentences. Use *will* for a promise or prediction. Use *be going to* for a plan.**

1. I promise. I_'ll_ call you tonight.
2. Lia has a plan. She ______________ take a vacation next month.
3. The newspaper predicts we ______________ have a long, hot summer.
4. Don't worry. I ______________ give you a ride.
5. Marta ______________ stay home and study tonight.
6. We think we ______________ have a test next week.

C Complete the predictions. Use *will* and the verbs in parentheses.

1. Many people are moving to the city. The city ____will build____ more apartments. (build)
2. Computers are important for many jobs. Schools ________________ more computer classes. (offer)
3. The roads are falling apart. The city ________________ the roads soon. (fix)
4. The price of gasoline is very high. People ________________ smaller cars. (buy)
5. People want to spend time outside. The city ________________ more parks and recreation areas. (plan)
6. There's a lot of garbage in the river. The city ________________ the river. (clean up)

D Complete the conversations with the correct forms of *be going to* or *will*. Use the cues in parentheses to help you.

1. **A:** What time ____are____ you ____going to____ leave for the airport? (plan)
   B: My brother ________________ pick me up at 7:00. (promise)
2. **A:** When ________________ you ________________ call me? (plan)
   B: I ________________ call at 9:00. (promise)
3. **A:** Where ________________ you ________________ be after class? (plan)
   B: I don't know. I ________________ wait for you at the coffee shop. (promise)
4. **A:** Who ________________ pick up the tickets for the concert? (promise)
   B: Carol ________________ get them. She works near the concert hall. (plan)
5. **A:** ________________ Simon and Thomas ________________ be at work tomorrow? (plan)
   B: No. They ________________ be at a meeting in Boston. (plan)
6. **A:** When ________________ you ________________ take me shopping? (plan)
   B: I ________________ take you after work. (promise)

LESSON 4 EVERYDAY CONVERSATION

A Complete the conversation. Use the words in the box.

See you	up to you	do you have in mind
~~Would you like to~~	I'll meet you	I think I'd rather

Sharon: Would you like to (1) get together this weekend?

Mike: Sure. What ______ (2)?

Sharon: Well, on Sunday there's a concert or a baseball game.

It's ______ (3).

Mike: ______ (4) go to the baseball game.

Sharon: OK. ______ (5) at the stadium at 12:30.

Mike: That sounds great. ______ (6) then.

B Complete the questions with *would rather.* Then answer the questions. Use your own information.

1. **A:** Would you rather eat out tonight or make something at home?
   B: I'd rather eat out.
2. **A:** ______ you ______ watch TV or take a walk?
   B: ______
3. **A:** ______ you ______ go swimming or play tennis?
   B: ______
4. **A:** ______ you ______ play football or play soccer?
   B: ______
5. **A:** ______ you ______ do your homework or do the dishes?
   B: ______
6. **A:** ______ you ______ dance or listen to music?
   B: ______

DO THE MATH Go to page 87.

A Read the article. What do people do for fun?

The *News of the Day* Entertainment Report: What Our Readers Do for Fun

People today are working more and more and relaxing less and less. It's important to work, but it's also important to have fun and relax. Having fun helps us rest and feel better.

So what do people do for fun? *News of the Day* asked 30 of our readers about their favorite fun activities.

Ten of our 30 readers, or 33%, say they like to read. They read because it's a great activity and they can do it anywhere at any time. All they need is a book, a magazine, or a newspaper. It doesn't take a lot of energy, and they can learn at the same time!

Eight of our 30 readers, or 26%, enjoy spending time with their families. They talk, visit, and play with each other.

Our other readers said that they enjoy using the computer, working in the garden, exercising, and walking. So when you can, do something fun. Relax. You'll feel better.

Reading	**33%**
Spending time with the family	**26%**
Using the computer	**20%**
Working in the garden	**10%**
Exercising	**7%**
Walking	**4%**

B Mark the sentences *T* (true) or *F* (false).

__F__ 1. Today, people spend less time working.

____ 2. It's important to spend time having fun.

____ 3. The most popular activity takes a lot of energy.

____ 4. Thirty percent of readers spend time with family.

____ 5. Twenty-five percent of readers exercise for fun.

____ 6. Ten percent of readers work in the garden.

A Read the conversation. Then underline examples of verbs with *will*, and circle examples of verbs with *be going to*.

Ivan: What are you going to do this afternoon?

Tina: We're going to see the new movie at the Town Theater. Do you want to come with us?

Ivan: No, thanks. We saw it last night. I bet you'll love it.

Tina: I think I will. The newspaper says it's a great movie.

Ivan: We're going to have a party for Olga's sister tonight. Why don't you come by after the movie?

Tina: What time?

Ivan: The party is going to start at about 8:00. We'll be in the backyard. Walk around to the back of the house when you get there.

Tina: OK. We'll stop by after the movie.

Ivan: Great. I'll see you tonight.

B Read the sentences. Check (✓) Plan, Promise, or Prediction.

	Plan	Promise	Prediction
1. What are you going to do?	✓		
2. We're going to see the new movie at the Town Theater.			
3. You'll love it.			
4. I think I will.			
5. We're going to have a party for Olga's sister tonight.			
6. The party is going to start at about 8:00.			
7. We'll be in the backyard.			
8. We'll stop by after the movie.			
9. I'll see you tonight.			

UNIT

3 A Job to Do

LESSON 1 VOCABULARY

A Look at the ad. Write the answers to the questions.

1. How much is the digital camera? It's $149.99.
2. How much is the headset? ____________
3. How much is the keyboard? ____________
4. How much is the CPU? ____________

B Who says these things? Write the job titles. Use the words in the box.

photographer	graphic designer	office manager	~~computer technician~~

1. "I need to fix this CPU and repair the system." computer technician
2. "Let me check my camera. OK, now, smile!" ____________
3. "I use my computer and graphics to design pictures." ____________
4. "I keep the office organized and everyone working on schedule." ____________

C Read the sentences. Match the underlined words with their meanings.

b 1. My computer crashed again!
____ 2. I need to close this window.
____ 3. There's a new virus in the system.
____ 4. I started my computer, but I don't see the desktop.

a. small area on the computer screen
b. stopped working
c. display on the monitor of programs and folders
d. a program that causes computer problems

LESSON 2 WRITING

A **Complete the email. Use the words in the box.**

are arriving late	must be at work by	are taking 30-minute	Break times
may not eat or drink	~~Steve Karra~~	are not cleaning their	Employee Policies

TO: allstaff@baineindustries.com

FROM: ___Steve Karra___(1), President

SUBJECT: ______________(2)

The managers are noticing some problems.

1. Some employees ______________(3) for work.
2. Some employees ______________(4) breaks.
3. Some employees ______________(5) work areas.

Please follow these company policies:

Employees ______________(6) 9:00 a.m.

Employees ______________(7) near computers.

______________(8) are from 11:00 to 11:15 and from 3:00 to 3:15.

B **Complete the sentences. Circle *a* or *b*.**

1. The email is for ____.
   (a.) all employees
   b. Steve Karra
2. The email is from ____.
   a. all employees
   b. Steve Karra
3. ____ are reporting some problems.
   a. The employees
   b. The managers
4. ____ arrive after 9:30 every day.
   a. Some people
   b. All the workers
5. ____ must clean their work areas.
   a. The managers
   b. The employees
6. There ____ every day.
   a. are two breaks
   b. is one break

A **Look at the chart. Then complete the sentences. Use the comparative form of the adjectives in parentheses.**

	Max-Sound Radio	Mini-Power Radio
Price	$194	$94
Weight	3 lbs.	1 lb.
Size	large	small
Number of radios sold this week	12	20
Reliable	yes	no

(not) as…as

1. The Mini-Power is not as expensive as the Max-Sound. (expensive)
2. The Mini-Power is ____________ the Max-Sound. (heavy)
3. The Max-Sound is ____________ the Mini-Power. (small)

(less…than / more…than)

4. The Mini-Power is ____________ the Max-Sound. (popular)
5. The Mini-Power is ____________ the Max-Sound. (expensive)
6. The Max-Sound is ____________ the Mini-Power. (reliable)

B **Which sentences have the same meaning? Circle *a* or *b*.**

1. Hal's computers are less expensive than Computer World's computers.
   a. Hal's computers are as expensive as Computer World's computers.
   (b.) Computer World's computers are more expensive than Hal's computers.
2. Hal's salespeople are not as friendly as Computer World's salespeople.
   a. Hal's salespeople are less friendly than Computer World's salespeople.
   b. Hal's salespeople are as friendly as Computer World's salespeople.
3. Computer World is more popular than Hal's.
   a. Hal's is as popular as Computer World.
   b. Hal's is less popular than Computer World.
4. Computer World's technicians are not as experienced as Hal's technicians.
   a. Computer World's technicians are more experienced than Hal's technicians.
   b. Computer World's technicians are less experienced than Hal's technicians.

C Look at the chart. Write the answers to the questions.

	Trans-Phone	Express Phone	Phone Anywhere
cheap	★	★★	★★★
light	★★	★★★	★
small	★	★★	★★★
popular	★★	★★★	★
reliable	★★★	★★	★

1. Which phone is the cheapest? Phone Anywhere is the cheapest.
2. Which phone is the lightest? ____________
3. Which phone is the smallest? ____________
4. Which phone is the least popular? ____________
5. Which phone is the most reliable? ____________
6. Which phone is the most popular? ____________

D Read the ad. Circle the correct words.

Cameras R Us
Grand Opening

The (newer / newest) [1] Cameras R Us opens this weekend in Springfield. Our new store is (larger / largest) [2] than any other store in town. Come see our new low prices!

- Our prices are (lower / lowest) [3] than the prices at Camera Stop or Camera Mart. Come see the service!
- Our salespeople are the (friendlier / friendliest) [4] salespeople in the city.
- We offer the (faster / fastest) [5] and (more complete / most complete) [6] service around.
- We are here to help you! Come and see for yourself!

A **Complete the conversation. Use the words in the box.**

You have to	is it	won't have to tell
most creative person	~~can I see you~~	good worker

Mr. Young: Charles, can I see you (1) for a minute?

Charles: Yes, Mr. Young. What ______ (2)?

Mr. Young: You're a ______ (3). You're the ______ (4) in the office.

Charles: Thanks, Mr. Young.

Mr. Young: But, you take very long breaks. ______ (5) come back from your breaks on time.

Charles: I'm sorry. You ______ (6) me again.

Mr. Young: Thank you, Charles.

B **Complete the sentences. Use the superlative form of the words in parentheses.**

1. Jack is not organized. He's the least organized person I know. (organized)
2. San is polite and kind to everybody. He's the ______ person in the office. (nice)
3. Everyone likes Paula. She's the ______ person in the company. (patient)
4. Azim never finishes his work on time. He's the ______ person in the office (efficient)
5. I'm looking at three different computers. One is definitely the ______ compared to the other two. (expensive)
6. This camera has the ______ amount of storage for photos. I really need a lot of storage! (large)
7. The winter solstice is the ______ day of the year. (short)

DO THE MATH Go to page 88.

A Read the email. What classes is Ralston providing?

To: employees@ralston.us
From: Maria Wilson, maria@ralston.us
Date: 11/14/19
RE: Learning and Training Classes

Learn more and earn more. Starting January 18, Ralston Radio is providing training classes for all of our employees in the Houston office. Classes are short (four weeks) and small (12 students in each class). We have many great teachers, too, so sign up soon!

Learn the newest technology and the latest skills to help you do a better job and prepare you for a better position at Ralston. Classes include:

- **Management Training:** Do you want to be an office manager? Come learn how to keep an office organized and in order. Learn how to make work schedules and supervise others.
- **Design Training:** If you're interested in graphic design, you should take this class. Learn how to make posters and brochures. You can use graphics to design pictures.
- **Computer Technology:** Do you want to be a computer technician? Take this class and learn about new computer programs. Learn how to fix CPUs and repair computer systems.

For more information email me at maria@ralston.us.

B Mark the sentences *T* (true), *F* (false), or *NI* (no information).

_F_ 1. These classes are only for managers.

____ 2. Maria Wilson teaches a class.

____ 3. The classes begin in January.

____ 4. In Design Training, you can learn how to supervise others.

____ 5. You can learn about designing pictures in Management Training.

____ 6. In Computer Technology, you can learn how to fix CPUs.

Look at the pictures. Then write sentences. Use the adjectives in parentheses with *not as...as* and *more...than* or *less...than*.

1. Leo

   (organized) Leo is not as organized as Rosa and Gloria.
   He is less organized than Rosa and Gloria.

   (efficient) ______________________________
   ____

   (reliable) ______________________________
   ____

2. Rosa

   (organized) ______________________________
   ____

   (efficient) ______________________________
   ____

   (reliable) ______________________________
   ____

3. Gloria

   (organized) ______________________________
   ____

   (efficient) ______________________________
   ____

   (reliable) ______________________________
   ____

UNIT

4 Good Work

LESSON 1 VOCABULARY

A **Look at the notes. Complete the chart.**

Interview with Amy Kim	Interview with Juan Perea
On time	Ten minutes late
Used cell phone	Didn't use cell phone
Dressed professionally	Dressed inappropriately
Forgot resume	Good resume
Not nervous	Nervous

	Amy Kim		Juan Perea	
Dos	**Yes**	**No**	**Yes**	**No**
Arrive on time	✓			✓
Dress appropriately				
Bring resume				
Do nots	**Yes**	**No**	**Yes**	**No**
Use cell phone				
Look nervous				

B **Who says these things? Match the statements with the types of worker.**

__b__ 1. Everyone says I have great ideas.
____ 2. I can fix any problem, big or small.
____ 3. I work well with other people.
____ 4. I don't need a lot of supervision. I can work on my own.
____ 5. I see what needs to be done, and then I do it!
____ 6. I'm good at showing people what to do and supervising others.

a. a self-starter
b. a creative thinker
c. a go-getter
d. a problem-solver
e. a good leader
f. a team player

A Complete the letter. Use the words in the box.

Sincerely	of accounts manager	learning more about
~~Dear Ms. Sopal~~	organization and communication	555-4114

Ms. Sopal, Personnel Manager
Linwood Communications Corp.
457 West Park Drive
Tampa, FL 33602

Dear Ms. Sopal (1):

Thank you for the opportunity to interview for the position ________ (2). I enjoyed ________ (3) your company. I hope to have the chance to use my ________ (4) skills at Linwood Communications. If you have any questions, or need more information, please call me at ________ (5). You can also email me at abecker@abc.us.

________ (6),

Alberto Becker

Alberto Becker

B Complete the sentences. Circle *a* or *b*.

1. ____ interviewed Alberto.
   - (a.) Ms. Sopal
   - b. Mr. Becker
2. Alberto applied for the ____ position.
   - a. personnel manager
   - b. accounts manager
3. Alberto has organization and ____ skills.
   - a. communication
   - b. interview
4. The interviewer can call Alberto at ____.
   - a. 555-4114
   - b. abecker@abc.us

A **Complete the sentences with the present perfect. Use the verbs in parentheses.**

1. Don ___has completed___ high school. (complete)
2. I ______________ English since last March. (study)
3. We ______________ interview questions several times. (practice)
4. Bonita ______________ three interviews in the past few weeks. (have)
5. My brother ______________ the problem with the car. (not fix)
6. Our neighbors ______________ here for ten years. (be)
7. Sophie ______________ them for two weeks. (not see)
8. They ______________ us to their home many times. (invite)

B **Complete the sentences with *for* or *since*.**

1. Cyrus has worked here ___for___ three months.
2. He hasn't been in class __________ last week.
3. We've been here __________ 2:00.
4. Has Lucy been at the library __________ two hours?
5. Linda has been my neighbor __________ several years.
6. She has lived here __________ ten years.
7. James and I have been married __________ January.
8. We haven't read the news __________ two days.

C Complete the sentences with the present perfect and *for* or *since*. Use the verbs in parentheses.

1. Li-Anh ___has lived___ in San Diego ___for___ three years. (live)
2. She ______________ in an office ______________ June 2014. (work)
3. She ______________ an office manager ______________ one year. (be)
4. She ______________ English ______________ 2015. (not study)
5. Li-Anh ______________ any letters ______________ May. (not write)
6. She ______________ five people ______________ 9:00 this morning. (interview)

D Read the sentences. Then circle the correct words.

1. Lisa has fixed computers for three years. She ((fixes) / doesn't fix) computers now.
2. Lisa and Arturo have lived in Chicago. They (live / don't live) in Chicago now.
3. They've lived in California since 2013. They (live / don't live) there now.
4. We've been sick for two days. We (feel / don't feel) sick now.
5. Our friends have visited New York. They (are / aren't) still there.

E Rewrite the sentences. Use the present perfect of the underlined verbs and *for* or *since*.

1. Emma works for the TV station. She started working there eight years ago.
   Emma has worked for the TV station for eight years.
2. Emma and Paul are married. They got married in 2002.
   ____
3. Paul doesn't study English now. He stopped studying last year.
   ____
4. They live in an apartment downtown. They started living there two months ago.
   ____
5. Paul works for Warwick Industries. He started working there in December.
   ____

LESSON 4 EVERYDAY CONVERSATION

A Complete the conversation. Use the words in the box.

Have you been	I've been	can do it	a good leader
I'm a fast	~~How long~~	for four	Why do you think

Ms. Seldon: ___How long___ (1) have you been a salesperson at Gibson's?

Luis: ________ (2) a salesperson here ________ (3) years.

Ms. Seldon: ________ (4) you should be the new sales manager?

Luis: I'm ________ (5). I want to teach other salespeople what I've learned.

Ms. Seldon: ________ (6) a manager before?

Luis: No, but ________ (7) learner, and I know I ________ (8).

Ms. Seldon: That's great, Luis.

B Underline the contractions. Write the subjects and the full forms of the verbs, including the past participles.

1. I've finished my work for today. ___I have finished___
2. He's worked at the store since May. ________
3. We haven't done the work. ________
4. She's gotten a new job. ________
5. She's been the teacher's assistant for two months. ________
6. The letter hasn't arrived. ________
7. They've had several interviews. ________
8. I haven't talked to the manager. ________

C Underline the present perfect forms that can be contracted. Write the contractions and the past participles.

1. I have eaten there many times. ___I've eaten___
2. He has gone to see his boss in her office. ________
3. They have finished their homework tonight. ________
4. We have taken many pictures. ________
5. She has worked there for about six years. ________

DO THE MATH Go to page 88.

A Read the article. What do you need to get a promotion?

How Do I Get That Promotion?

How do you let your supervisor know that you have the skills for that promotion? You need to show your supervisor that you're ready for a promotion. Tell your supervisor what you can do. Most supervisors are looking for people with good communication skills, problem-solving skills, teamwork skills, flexibility, and creativity.

How are your communication skills?

- Are you a good listener?
- Can you give instructions or explain something to another person?

Tell your supervisor about these experiences.

How are you at solving problems?
What do you do when there is a problem?

- Do you study what happened?
- Do you find out what caused the problem?
- Do you try different things to correct the problem?

Tell your supervisor how you solved some problems.

How are you at working with others?

- Do you like working on projects in a group?
- Do you share your ideas in a group?
- Do you help others in a group?

Talk about groups you have worked with. Give examples of your teamwork skills.

Are you flexible? Creative?

- Do you try new ways to do your work?
- Do you like learning new things at work?
- Do you ever change the way you work?

When you talk to your supervisor, be specific. Talk about what you have done. Talk about what you can do for the company. Explain why you should get the promotion!

B Mark the sentences *T* (true), *F* (false), or *NI* (no information).

_T_ 1. To get a promotion, tell your supervisor what you can do.

____ 2. Supervisors don't care about good communication skills.

____ 3. It's a good idea to study why problems happen.

____ 4. It's not important to try different things to correct a problem.

____ 5. You shouldn't share ideas with other employees.

____ 6. Don't worry about good teamwork skills.

____ 7. It's important to try different ways to do work.

____ 8. Flexible employees get promoted 25% of the time.

A Read the article in the company news.

Blue Skies Music

WEEKLY NEWS

New Business Manager

Congratulations to Nick Sato on his promotion to business manager. Nick has been at Blue Skies Music for eight years. We are pleased that he is now leading the business department.

Al Gonzales, president of Blue Skies, says that Nick has great communication skills. "I've seen Nick do great things at Blue Skies. He listens to people, and he cares about them. He's trained many of our new employees in the basics. He's an excellent person to manage the business department."

One of Nick's new jobs will be to organize a problem-solving team. Nick has done a lot of work with problem solving. Nick said, "I've worked on two very interesting team projects since I started at Blue Skies. We've made some big changes since then, and I think things are working better now." He also said, "I haven't had time to talk to everyone in the business department, but I hope to talk to all of them soon."

With Nick's skills in problem solving and teamwork, we look forward to great things from the business department.

B Complete the tasks.

1. One example of the present perfect is underlined. Underline six more examples of the present perfect in the article.
2. Find the sentence with *for* and a period of time. Write it here.

   ____

3. Find the two sentences with since and a time when an activity began. Write them here.

   ____

   ____

4. Find the contractions in the article. Rewrite them using the full forms of the verbs.

   ______________ ______________

   ______________ ______________

   ______________ ______________

Community Resources

LESSON 1 VOCABULARY

A **Match the sentences with the community resources.**

<u>b</u> 1. I need to take a job-training class.
____ 2. I need low-cost health services.
____ 3. I need to bring in my cans and bottles.
____ 4. I'm 65 years old, and I want to take a class.
____ 5. I need to find government offices.
____ 6. I lost my cat, and I want to find it.

a. animal shelter
b. employment agency
c. senior center
d. recycling center
e. city hall
f. community clinic

B **Complete the flyer. Use the words in the box.**

volunteer programs	open house	wellness checkup	~~job fair~~	pet adoption

A Complete the email. Use the words in the box.

discussed the problem	~~on behalf of the students~~	invite you to visit
can see the problem	about a safety issue	are broken windows

To: Board Member Edwin Peterson <edwin.peterson@newcityschools.gov>
Re: Safety problem in our school

Dear Board Member Peterson,

I am writing to the school board __on behalf of the students__ (1) in my English class. We are worried ________ (2). The problem is that there ________ (3) in our classroom.

We are worried about broken glass and cold air in the winter. We've ________ (4) with our school principal, but she says there is no money for repairs right now.

We ________ (5) our school, so you ________ (6).
We hope you can help us make our school safe.

Sincerely,

Chu Pheng

B Match the pictures with the problems.

a

b

c

d

__c__ 1. The recycling center is closed.

____ 2. There is no stop sign.

____ 3. The windows are broken.

____ 4. The pipe is leaking.

A **Write *yes/no* questions. Use the present perfect.**

1. you / fix / the door
   Have you fixed the door?
2. Diana / paint / the apartment
   ____
3. Kevin / repair / the broken windows
   ____
4. Leo and Chan / be / to the animal shelter
   ____
5. you / write / a letter to the school board
   ____
6. they / take / a job-training class
   ____
7. the children / have / a wellness checkup
   ____
8. we / discuss / all the problems
   ____

B **Read the sentences. Circle the correct words.**

1. Have you (ever / yet) done any volunteer work?
2. I've (yet / already) taken the cans to the recycling center.
3. We haven't gone to the senior center (ever / yet).
4. Has Larry (yet / ever) volunteered at the animal shelter?
5. He's (ever / already) helped in his community garden.
6. I haven't gone to the job fair (already / yet).
7. Have Roberto and Ana (ever / yet) visited city hall?
8. Sally has (already / ever) been to the recreation center.

C Match the questions with the answers.

__c__ 1. Have you ever been to New York?

____ 2. Has Don ever studied another language?

____ 3. Have Luis and Marcos already signed up to volunteer?

____ 4. Has Marie already fixed the computer?

____ 5. Has Mark made dinner yet?

a. No, he'll study French next semester.

b. No, she hasn't fixed it yet.

c. Yes, I went there last month.

d. Yes, he made it an hour ago.

e. Yes, they did that yesterday.

D Look at the picture. Write sentences about Ramiro.

Things Ramiro has done:

1. Ramiro has already mixed the paint.
2. ______________________________
3. ______________________________

Things Ramiro hasn't done:

4. Ramiro hasn't cleaned the floor yet.
5. ______________________________
6. ______________________________

A Complete the conversation. Use the words in the box.

calling about	like to know
help with meals	Sign me up
what kinds of things	can I help you
complete a short training session	

A: Springfield Senior Center. How ___can I help you___ (1)?

B: Hi. I'm ______________ (2) the volunteer training.

A: Sure. What would you ______________ (3)?

B: I'm interested in learning about ______________ (4) the volunteers do.

A: Some volunteers help entertain the residents. Others ______________ (5).

B: Oh, I'd love to help with the meals.

A: Great! You need to ______________ (6), and then you can decide when you want to volunteer.

B: Sounds good. ______________ (7)!

B Read the sentences. Circle the correct words.

1. Have you ever (been / was) to a community meeting?
2. Maggie didn't (go / gone) to the meeting yesterday.
3. She has (had / have) a cold for two days.
4. Did Tam (volunteer / volunteered) to help?
5. We haven't (sign / signed) up to be volunteers.
6. Phuong has (go / gone) to the clinic three times.
7. Marcos didn't (signed / sign) the application form.

DO THE MATH Go to page 89.

A Read the flyer. How can you help the environment?

Keep Our State Beautiful

This group started in 2001 to protect the environment.

Litter Pickers

organizes volunteers to pick up trash in public places. For information or to volunteer, call 555-9944.

State Parks Program

Help clean up the parks in our state. Last year our volunteers picked up more than 10,000 pounds of trash! You can make a difference. **Call 555-3333 today.**

No Pollution Now

Now you can report pollution problems when you see them. If you see litter, water pollution, or other environmental problems, let us know and we'll check it out.[1] **Call us: 555-1000.**

Community Improvement Grants[2]

Does your community need money for an environmental project? If so, Community Improvement Grants may be the answer. We help programs that want to stop littering, protect our natural resources, and make our communities beautiful. Call Paula at 555-2626.

[1] check it out: find out more information about it
[2] grant: a gift of money for a specific use

B Mark the sentences *T* (true), *F* (false), or *NI* (no information).

_F_ 1. Litter Pickers pays people to pick up litter.

____ 2. Last year, volunteers for the State Parks Program picked up over 10,000 pounds of trash.

____ 3. Litter Pickers will pick up trash at your house.

____ 4. Many people volunteer for No Pollution Now.

____ 5. Community Improvement Grants will help programs that want to stop littering.

____ 6. Community Improvement Grants provided over $15,000 to the community last year.

A **Read the questionnaire. Then answer the question.**

NAME: CLARA

Have you ever...	YES	NO
1. taken things to a recycling center?	✓	
2. written a letter about a problem?		✓
3. volunteered to clean up trash?	✓	
4. volunteered for a local organization		✓
5. planted trees in your community?	✓	
6. gone to a community meeting?		✓
7. celebrated Earth Day?	✓	
8. reported problems in your community?		✓

If you answered "yes" to questions 1, 3, 5, or 7, you should volunteer for the **Clean Up Now** program.
If you answered "yes" to questions 2, 4, 6, or 8, you should volunteer for the **Make a Difference** program.

Should Clara volunteer for "Clean Up Now" or "Make a Difference"?

____

B **Look at A. Write sentences about Clara.**

Things Clara has done:

1. Clara has taken things to a recycling center.
2. ______________________________
3. ______________________________
4. ______________________________

Things Clara hasn't done:

5. Clara hasn't written a letter about a problem.
6. ______________________________
7. ______________________________
8. ______________________________

UNIT 6

What's Cooking?

LESSON 1 VOCABULARY

A Match the pictures with the words.

____ glass	__2__ boil	____ knife	____ chop	____ plate
____ utensils	____ pour	____ stir	____ pot	____ bowl

B Complete the sentences. Use the words in the box.

grater	steamer	slicer	mixer	~~peeler~~	beater

1. I want to peel the potatoes. Do you have a __peeler__?
2. We need to grate the cheese. Do you have the ____________?
3. I'll mix the eggs and sugar. Do you have the ____________?
4. I like steamed vegetables, so I bought a new ____________.
5. Can you slice the bread? Here's the ____________.
6. You need to beat the eggs for a long time. Use the ____________.

LESSON 2 WRITING

A Complete the story. Use the words in the box.

to the supermarket	stirred everything	away the groceries
~~was the best cook~~	in the oven	and peeled it

My Favorite Dish

When I was a child in Russia, my aunt Tanya was the best cook (1) in the family. Every Saturday, we went ________ (2). She always bought the freshest fruit. At home, she got things ready while I put ________ (3).

Aunt Tanya's fruit cake was my favorite dish. First, she washed the fruit ________ (4). Then she put all the other ingredients in a bowl, and I ________ (5) together. Finally, she put the cake ________ (6) and baked it.

B Put the sentences in the correct order.

Rosa's Recipe for Banana Bread

____ Put the pan in the oven and cook for 45 minutes.

1 Take 4 bananas and peel them.

____ Stir everything together and pour into a pan.

____ Cut up the bananas.

____ Put the bananas in a bowl with 2 eggs, 2 cups of flour, and 1 cup of sugar.

____ Take the bread out of the oven. Let cool and eat!

C Rewrite the recipe. Use as many sequencing words in the box as you can.

first	later	then	finally	lastly	next

Rosa's Recipe for Banana Bread

First, take 4 bananas and peel them.

A **Read the recipe. Circle the correct words.**

Pizza Recipe
1. Take a bowl. Put ((in) / on) flour and the other ingredients.
2. Don't leave (out / off) the salt. Stir it.
3. Chop (up / off) some vegetables.
4. Put them (on / in) the pizza.
5. Turn (in / on) the oven. Bake the pizza for 25 minutes.
6. Take (up / out) the pizza and eat it.

B **Read the sentences. Separate the phrasal verbs. Then write the sentences another way. Use the pronouns *it* or *them* for the underlined words.**

1. I'll chop up <u>the carrots.</u>
   I'll chop them up.
2. Can you figure out <u>these recipes?</u>
   ____
3. Did you pick up <u>the milk</u> on your way home?
   ____
4. I didn't write down <u>the ingredients.</u>
   ____
5. I think we can turn off <u>the stove</u> now.
   ____
6. Did you turn on <u>the oven?</u>
   ____
7. I won't leave out <u>the sugar</u> next time.
   ____
8. Did you put in <u>the eggs</u>?
   ____

C Match the questions with the answers.

c 1. Did you start the car?	a. Yes, I wrote them down.
____ 2. Did you find the answer?	b. Yes, I picked them up.
____ 3. Did you forget to add the milk?	c. Yes, I turned it on.
____ 4. Did you buy the newspapers?	d. Yes, I put them in.
____ 5. Did you copy the phone numbers?	e. Yes, I left it out.
____ 6. Did you add the apples?	f. Yes, I figured it out.

D Complete the sentences. Use the words in the box.

for	over	on	~~off~~	after

1. This is our stop. We have to get ____off____ the bus now.
2. Pam is away on vacation, so I'm looking ________ her cat.
3. I can't find my keys. I have to look ________ them.
4. Do you want to come ________ for dinner next weekend?
5. I'm tired of walking. Let's get ________ the bus.

E Complete the sentences. Use the correct pronouns for the underlined words.

1. Did <u>Amalia</u> write down <u>the address</u>?

   Yes, ____she wrote it down____.
2. Did <u>Fred</u> look for <u>the phone numbers</u>?

   Yes, ________________.
3. Did <u>Mario and you</u> turn off <u>the computer</u>?

   Yes, ________________.
4. Did <u>Bernard</u> figure out <u>the answers</u>?

   Yes, ________________.
5. Did <u>Marissa</u> get over <u>her cold</u>?

   Yes, ________________.
6. Did <u>George and Franco</u> pick up <u>the cake</u>?

   Yes, ________________.

LESSON 4 EVERYDAY CONVERSATION

A Complete the conversation. Use the words in the box.

cut down on	have a question	~~Excuse me~~
try them	are the best	chef doesn't use

Elena: ___Excuse me___(1). I ________(2) about something on the menu. What are your special French fries?

Waiter: We use two different kinds of potatoes.

Elena: Are they very salty?

Waiter: No, the ________(3) much salt.

Elena: Good. I'm trying to ________(4) salt. I'll ________(5).

Waiter: Excellent choice. Ours ________(6) in town.

B Circle the correct possessive adjectives or possessive pronouns.

1. Mai and Anna are looking for (theirs / (their)) recipes.
2. I have (your / yours). Do you have (my / mine)?
3. (Her / Hers) sandwich was delicious. (Our / Ours) were too spicy.
4. How was (your / yours) soup?
5. Gabriela didn't finish (her / hers) soup. Did Luz finish (her / hers)?
6. (My / Mine) name is Katrina. What's (your / yours)?

C Complete the conversation. Use the words in the box.

have to tip	their service good	stay there to work
the restaurants should pay	don't get paid	~~why Americans tip~~

Jonas: I don't understand ___why Americans tip___(1).

Margie: Why not? Waiters work hard, but they ________(2) much.

Jonas: I know, but I think ________(3) them more. Then we don't ________(4).

Margie: Some restaurants do that, but most don't. Our favorite restaurant doesn't allow tips.

Jonas: Really? Is ________(5)?

Margie: Yes, it is. And the waiters ________(6) instead of finding a better job.

DO THE MATH Go to page 90.

A **Read the article. What makes food unsafe?**

Unsafe Food Problems in Greenville Last Year

Population of Greenville 29,800

Dr. Peter Jeffords, head of Greenville Hospital, said today that he is worried about the large number of people in the town of Greenville who got sick last year from unsafe food. "It's a problem everywhere," said Dr. Jeffords. "In fact, much of the U.S. population gets sick from unsafe food every year." Most of these problems are not serious, but some people can get very sick and need to go to the hospital. A very small percentage of people die from bacteria and food poisoning every year. Children under five years old and adults over 65 are more likely than other people to get sick.

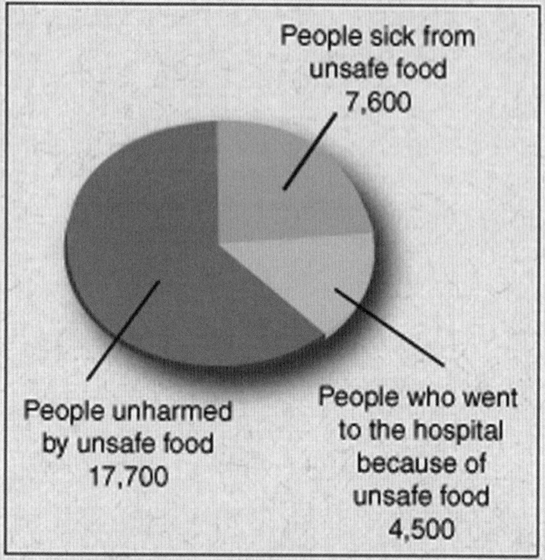

We asked Dr. Jeffords what we can do to stay safe. He told us. You can have fun in the kitchen and enjoy your food if you follow these rules:

- Wash your hands.
- Work on a clean counter, and always use clean dishes.
- Don't work with food when you are sick.
- Don't touch uncooked food with your hands.
- Keep food at safe temperatures. Keep cold food below 41°F. Keep hot food over 140°F.
- Check the "use by" dates. Throw out food that looks or smells bad.

B **Mark the sentences *T* (true) or *F* (false).**

__T__ 1. Every year much of the U.S. population gets sick from food-related diseases.

____ 2. Young children and older adults are more likely to get sick than the rest of the population.

____ 3. It is always safe to keep cold food below 41°F.

____ 4. Some people who get sick from unsafe food have to go to the hospital.

____ 5. It's okay to work with food when you're sick.

____ 6. When food looks or smells bad, it's okay to cook it.

A Read the essay.

The Best Chicken Soup in Town

I love to make chicken soup. Once a month, I make a shopping list and write down the ingredients I need. I always look for the freshest vegetables. I like to put them in the soup.

When I get home from the supermarket, I check my ingredients carefully. I don't want to leave anything out. First, I put the chicken in a big pot of hot water and let it cook. Then I chop up onions, carrots, and celery. Next, I put them in and stir everything together. Finally, I add noodles or rice.

When I make my chicken soup, I usually invite my friends to come over to my house for dinner. They say that mine is the best chicken soup in town!

B Complete the tasks.

1. Find three sentences in the essay with separable phrasal verbs. Then write the verbs here.

   write down____________________________________

   ____

   ____

2. Find one sentence in the article with two separable phrasal verbs. Then write it here.

   ____

3. Find two sentences in the article with inseparable phrasal verbs. Then write them here.

   ____

   ____

4. Find a possessive adjective in the article. Then write it here.

   ____

5. Find a possessive pronoun in the article. Then write it here.

   ____

6. Find four sequencing words in the article. Then write them here.

   ____

UNIT 7

Money Wise

LESSON 1 VOCABULARY

A Look at the pictures. Match the pictures with the words.

____ security guard

____ desk teller

__1__ teller window

____ loan officer

____ account services desk

____ open an account

____ apply for a loan

____ accounts manager

B Complete the conversations. Use the words in the box.

~~joint account~~	savings account	online banking	direct deposit

1. **Customer:** My wife and I want to share a checking account.
   Accounts Manager: Then you need a ______joint account______.
2. **Customer:** I want to use banking services from my home computer.
   Accounts Manager: That's easy! You can use ____________________.
3. **Customer:** I want to save money to buy a house.
   Accounts Manager: You should open a ____________________.
4. **Customer:** I want my paycheck to go directly into my account.
   Accounts Manager: You need ____________________.

A Complete the essay. Use the words in the box.

save money in	~~is hoping to buy~~	cheaper to bring
reach his goal	financial planning	plans his shopping
doesn't buy lunch	share the cost	

My Brother's Financial Planning

by Luisa Ruiz

My brother Miguel ___is hoping to buy___(1) a new computer in six months. His old one works, but it is very slow. Miguel needs a faster computer because he wants to take some online classes. Miguel has a plan. He has already started to ________(2) his account at the bank. I also gave him some ideas to help with his ________(3).

Miguel has learned a lot about saving money. Since he rides to work with me now, we ________(4) of gas. He ________(5) at work anymore. Now he makes his own lunch because it's ________(6) it from home. Miguel also ________(7) carefully. He makes a list of the things he wants. He also uses coupons to save money. Saving money isn't easy, but his financial plan is working. Soon Miguel will ________(8) and get a new computer.

B Mark the sentences *T* (true), *F* (false), or *NI* (no information).

__T__ 1. Luisa's brother wants a new computer.

____ 2. Miguel doesn't have a financial plan.

____ 3. Luisa has a new computer.

____ 4. Miguel doesn't have a bank account.

____ 5. Luisa and Miguel ride to work together.

____ 6. Miguel buys lunch at work.

____ 7. Luisa also makes shopping lists.

____ 8. Miguel's financial plan is working.

A Match the *if* clauses with the main clauses.

_d_ 1. If I have enough money,	a. if we need some food.
____ 2. Ernesto will open a bank account	b. she will have $480 in a year.
____ 3. We will go shopping	c. if it doesn't work well.
____ 4. If Anne saves $40 every month,	d. I will buy a new coat.
____ 5. If the sale begins today,	e. if he wants to save money.
____ 6. They won't buy the car	f. we won't pay the full price.

B Complete the conversation with the real conditional. Use the verbs in parentheses.

Marta: You know, if I ___get___(1) that job, I ___'ll need___(2) a jacket. (get, need)

Tanya: This jacket is nice. Try it on. If it __________(3), I __________(4) a larger size. (not fit, look for)

Marta: Oh, it's too small. I need a medium.

Tanya: Here's a medium gray jacket and a medium black one.

Marta: I like the gray one, but it's expensive. I __________(5) it if it __________(6) on sale. (buy, be)

Tanya: Oh, look! It's on sale. And if you __________(7) your credit card, you __________(8) even more! (use, save)

C Complete the conversations. Use the words in parentheses.

1. **A:** What will you buy if there's a sale this weekend?
   B: ___I'll buy a new camera___ if there's a sale. (new camera)
2. **A:** How much money will you need if you buy the camera?
   B: ____________________ if I buy the camera. ($200)
3. **A:** How will you pay for the camera if you buy it?
   B: If I buy it, ____________________. (use a check)
4. **A:** What will you do if you get the camera?
   B: If I get it, ____________________. (take pictures in the park)

D Read the conversations. Complete the questions.

1. **A:** What will Chris do if he gets a better job?

   B: If Chris gets a better job, he'll save more money.

2. **A:** What will he do ______________________________?

   B: If he saves money, he'll buy a computer.

3. **A:** What will Sara do ______________________________?

   B: If Sara has trouble with her car, she'll look for a new one.

4. **A:** What will we do ______________________________?

   B: If we find a good car, we'll ask about a car loan.

5. **A:** What will you do ______________________________?

   B: If I buy a new house, I'll sell the old one.

E Write sentences with the real conditional and *and*. Use the information in the chart.

If...	Mike	Luc
it rains tomorrow	go shopping	stay home
they take a long vacation	travel to South America	drive across the U.S.
they win $1,000	buy a new bicycle	open a savings account
the car doesn't work	ride his bicycle	fix the car
they stay home this weekend	clean the house	make dinner for his friends
there's a sale	not buy anything	buy a cell phone

1. If it rains tomorrow, Mike will go shopping and Luc will stay home.
2. ______________________________
3. ______________________________
4. ______________________________
5. ______________________________
6. ______________________________

A Complete the conversation. Use the words in the box.

before we send	talk to my supervisor	~~to report a problem~~
can I help you	that's impossible	When you receive

Sonia: I'm calling to report a problem (1) on my credit-card bill.

Customer Service: How ______ (2)?

Sonia: It says I spent $300 at Computer Town Electronics, but ______ (3). I didn't buy anything there.

Customer Service: OK. I'll ______ (4) and ask her to review it ______ (5) your next statement.

Sonia: So I don't have to pay the charges this month?

Customer Service: No. Let's wait and see. ______ (6) your next statement, you'll see your new balance.

B Read the sentences. Circle the correct words.

1. I will check the bank statement (before / when) it comes in the mail.
2. We will pay the bill (after / before) we check it.
3. (Before / After) we sign the check, we can get the money.
4. (If / Before) I make a mistake, I'll correct it.
5. In the restaurant, we pay (when / after) we eat.
6. I can save money at the store (if / before) I use coupons.

C Match the clauses to make sentences.

b	1. When the bank opens	a. when she needs money.
____	2. She'll make a withdrawal	b. I'll make a deposit.
____	3. They'll get a bill	c. after I open an account.
____	4. I'll get some checks	d. before they need to pay.

DO THE MATH Go to page 90.

LESSON 5 READING

A **Read the article. How can you avoid identity theft?**

Identity Theft at Bank Central

Lakewood—For six months, Noreen Smith, a teller at Bank Central, used her computer to steal bank customers' personal information. Smith then used the information to make credit card purchases. When the bank manager stopped her, she was carrying papers with the names, social security numbers, and credit card numbers of several Bank Central customers.

Lakewood mayor Paul Nelson said, "Identity theft is a growing problem in Lakewood and across the U.S. Everyone needs to be careful. This is happening more often."

Mayor Nelson says we should all do the following things to protect ourselves:

1. Shred, or cut up, papers with your bank account numbers and bills with your personal information.
2. Don't carry your social security card with you. Don't give people your social security number if it isn't really needed.
3. Don't give your personal information on the phone or over the Internet if you don't know the person.
4. Keep your social security card and credit cards in a safe place at home.

Mayor Nelson said, "The bank is telling all its customers to check their accounts carefully. We want to make sure everyone's information is safe."

B **Complete the sentences. Circle *a* or *b*.**

1. Noreen Smith used her computer to get bank customers' ____.
   a. credit cards
   (b.) personal information
2. Smith had ____ with her when the bank manager stopped her.
   a. papers with names and numbers
   b. credit card purchases
3. In the article, ____ is talking about identify theft.
   a. the bank manager
   b. the mayor
4. Identify theft is a problem that is getting ____.
   a. smaller
   b. bigger
5. People should keep their social security cards and credit cards ____.
   a. with them
   b. in a safe place
6. The article ____ people ways to keep their personal information safe.
   a. tells
   b. doesn't tell

Look at the pictures. Write sentences with the real conditional. Use the words in parentheses.

1. If Enrique , then he .

(save money) (buy a car)

If Enrique saves money, he'll buy a car.

2. If he , then he .

(buy a car) (drive to California)

____

3. If he 

, then he .

(drive to California) (need more money)

____

4. If he , then he .

(need more money) (need another job)

____

5. If he , then he .

(need another job) (look in the want ads)

____

6. If he 

, then he .

(look in the want ads) (get a better job)

____

UNIT

8 Living Well

LESSON 1 VOCABULARY

A Look at the pictures. Match the pictures with the words.

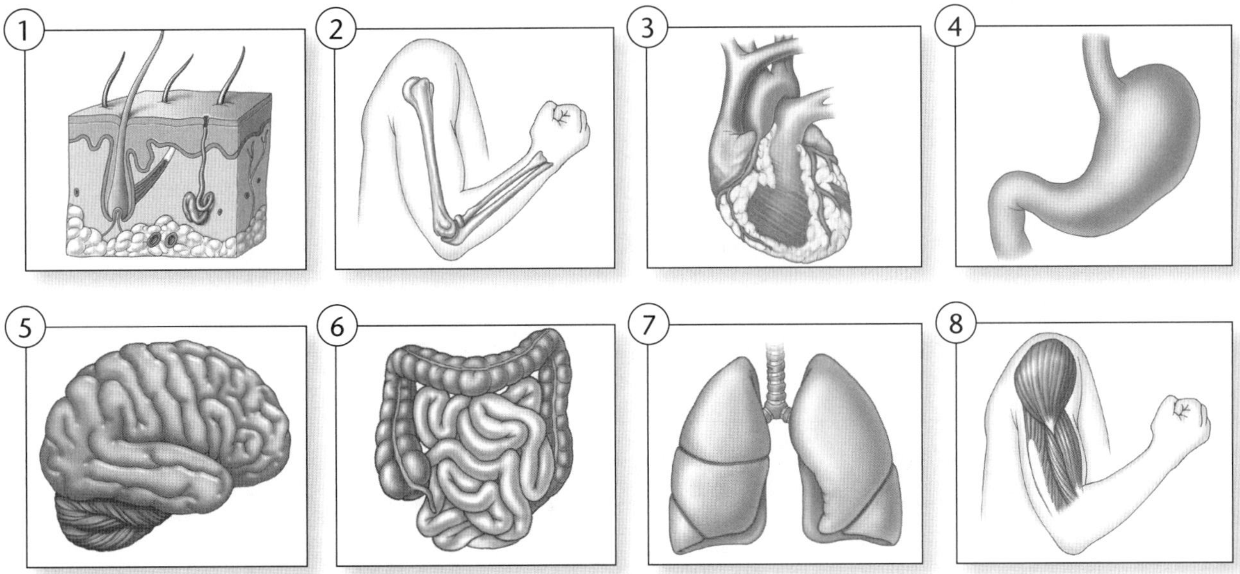

____	heart	____	stomach	____	bones	__1__	skin
____	brain	____	lungs	____	muscles	____	intestines

B Match the statements with the hospital department names.

__b__ 1. Could you check on Mr. Allison in room 224? It's time for his medicine.

____ 2. Congratulations! You have a baby girl!

____ 3. Mrs. Patel, your son has a bad cold. I'll give him some medicine.

____ 4. We're going to do some tests to check your heart.

____ 5. The ambulance is arriving from the car accident!

____ 6. We'll take some X-rays of your arm and see if it is broken.

a. cardiology

b. nurse's station

c. emergency

d. pediatrics

e. maternity

f. radiology

A **Complete the outline. Use the sentences in the box. Use capital letters.**

Get in Shape	Manage Stress	See the dentist for cleanings
Lift weights	~~Eat low-fat food~~	Make medical and dental appointments

Wellness Plan

I. Improve Eating Habits
   A. Eat less fast food
   B. Eat low-fat food (1)
   C. Eat more fruit and vegetables

II. ______ (2)
   A. Go swimming three times a week
   B. ______ (3)

III. Stay Well
   A. ______ (4)
      1. See the doctor for a physical exam
      2. ______ (5)
   B. ______ (6)

B **Look at the outline in A. Where do these points belong? Write *I, II,* or *III.***

I 1. Eat apples, carrots, and lettuce.
____ 2. Don't worry too much about little things.
____ 3. Play some sports.
____ 4. Follow your doctor's advice.
____ 5. Take a long walk.
____ 6. Don't eat too many hamburgers or French fries.
____ 7. Relax sometimes.
____ 8. Exercise several times a week.

A **Read the paragraph. Underline the examples of *used to*.**

My cousin Julia is in great shape now, but she wasn't in the past. She used to be very sick and tired all the time. She didn't use to eat three meals a day. Sometimes she only ate once a day! She used to eat out often, but now she makes her own meals at home. She really enjoys cooking now. Julia didn't like sports, so she didn't use to exercise much. Now, she runs or jogs every morning. She's not tired anymore. She used to look sad and worried, but now she's happy. She used to think that exercise was boring, but she doesn't now. She's healthy and happy. She feels great.

B **Read the sentences about what Julia does now but didn't do in the past. Write sentences with the correct forms of *used to*.**

1. Julia exercises a lot.
   Julia didn't use to exercise a lot.
2. She doesn't watch TV all the time.
   ____
3. She eats salads.
   ____
4. She doesn't eat a lot of junk food.
   ____
5. She doesn't stay inside all day.
   ____
6. She works outside.
   ____

C **Read the conversations. Complete the answers.**

1. **A:** Did Bob use to work in Boston?
   B: Yes, he used to work in Boston.
2. **A:** Did he use to take the subway to school?
   B: No, ____________________.
3. **A:** Did your friends use to live near here?
   B: Yes, ____________________.
4. **A:** Did they use to play sports?
   B: No, ____________________.
5. **A:** Did you use to take a walk every day?
   B: Yes, ____________________.
6. **A:** Did you use to get enough sleep?
   B: No, ____________________.

D Complete the questions. Use the correct form of *used to* and the words in parentheses.

1. Where did Rafael use to play tennis? (Rafael/play tennis)
2. How often ____________________? (he/practice)
3. Where ____________________? (Liz/exercise)
4. What ____________________? (you/eat for lunch)
5. How often ____________________? (you/go to the gym)
6. Why ____________________? (Katya/eat fast food)
7. Where ____________________? (Joe/study)
8. How ____________________? (Lara/save money)

E Complete the sentences. Use the simple past or *used to* and the verbs in parentheses.

1. I watched TV yesterday. (watch)
   I used to watch TV every night when I was younger.
2. I ____________________ my bike to school last week. (ride)
   I ____________________ my bike to school every day when I was younger.
3. I ____________________ only one cup of coffee this morning. (drink)
   I ____________________ four cups of coffee every day.
4. I ____________________ soccer with my friends last Saturday. (not play)
   I ____________________ soccer in high school.
5. I ____________________ to bed early last night. (go)
   I ____________________ to bed early when I was ten years old.
6. I ____________________ for the grammar test on Monday. (not study)
   I ____________________ for tests in high school.
7. I ____________________ this week. (not exercise)
   I ____________________ every day in college.
8. I ____________________ pizza for lunch today. (eat)
   I ____________________ pizza a lot last year.

A Complete the conversation. Use the words in the box.

under a lot of	Why don't you	~~a little concerned about~~	to join you
give it a try	I used to go	Have you been getting	invite them to walk

Dr. Stetson: I'm _a little concerned about_ (1) your blood pressure.

Mrs. Choi: I've been ____________ (2) stress recently.

Dr. Stetson: ____________ (3) enough sleep?

Mrs. Choi: Well, doctor, ____________ (4) to bed early, but now I just can't sleep.

Dr. Stetson: ____________ (5) walk after dinner?

Mrs. Choi: OK. I'll ____________ (6). I'll start tonight.

Dr. Stetson: Ask your family ____________ (7) on your walk.

Mrs. Choi: That's a good idea! I'll ____________ (8) with me. Thanks!

B Complete the sentences with the present perfect continuous. Use the words in parentheses.

1. Mrs. Choi _has been sleeping_ better since she saw the doctor. (sleep)
2. She ____________ as stressed. (not feel)
3. She and her husband ____________ every night after dinner. (walk)
4. Her children ____________ about how well she looks. (talk)
5. Her husband ____________ happier. (act)
6. He ____________ more sleep too. (get)
7. He ____________ more productively, so he is less stressed. (work)

DO THE MATH Go to page 91.

A Read the prescription label. What kind of information can you find on it?

Rx **Medi-Center Pharmacy**
20 Central Street
Dallas, TX 75231
Telephone: 203-555-2569

KEEP OUT OF REACH OF CHILDREN

RX 2211438 Dr. Cohen, Robert
Walker, Lisa 08/23/17

TAKE 1 TEASPOON EVERY 4 HOURS AS NEEDED.

60 ml
Roxicet Soln 5 mg/325/5ml

NO REFILLS Expiration date: 08/23/18

CAUTION: This medication can make you sleepy.
It may cause headaches.

Do not take more than the dosage listed.

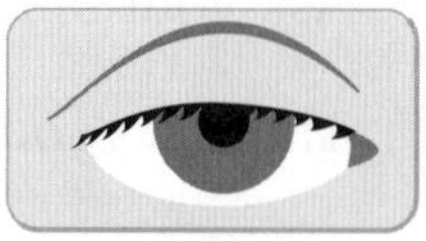

B Mark the sentences *T* (true), *F* (false), or *NI* (no information).

__F__ 1. The prescription number is 203555-2569
____ 2. The medicine is for Lisa Walker.
____ 3. She can take one teaspoon every four hours.
____ 4. She needs to eat something before she takes the medicine.
____ 5. She can get one refill of this medicine.
____ 6. The medicine may make her sleepy.
____ 7. This is a generic medicine.
____ 8. The medicine is safe for children.

UNIT 8 ANOTHER LOOK

A **Write answers to the questions. Use the correct form of *used to* and your own information.**

When you were eight years old, what did you do?

1. What school did you use to go to?
   I used to go to Belleville Primary School.
2. What programs did you use to watch on TV?
   ____
3. What games did you and your friends use to play together?
   ____
4. How did you use to get to school?
   ____
5. What time did you use to get up in the morning?
   ____
6. What time did you use to go to bed at night?
   ____
7. Where did you use to go on vacation?
   ____
8. What did you use to do on vacations?
   ____
9. What sports did you use to play?
   ____
10. Who used to be your favorite singer?
    ____

B **Look at your answers in A. Choose one answer and write a paragraph on your own paper about what you used to do.**

When I was eight years old, I used to go on vacations with my family. We used to travel to my grandmother's house in Miami ...

UNIT 9

Hit the Road

LESSON 1 VOCABULARY

A Match the pictures with the words.

____ headlight	____ license plate	____ windshield	____ tire	__1__ hood
____ trunk	____ gas tank	____ steering wheel	____ horn	____ bumper

B Match the sentences with the parts of the car.

__c__ 1. Your owner's manual is in here.

____ 2. Use this to see if anyone is behind you.

____ 3. This will show you how fast you are going.

____ 4. Keep both hands on it when you're driving.

____ 5. Use this to warn other drivers if they don't see you.

____ 6. Put the key in this to start the car.

a. speedometer

b. steering wheel

c. glove compartment

d. horn

e. ignition

f. rearview mirror

A Complete the story. Use the words in the box.

be sure to take	take my advice	~~like to travel~~
stayed there for two	be ready to	we took a train trip
you can see	and comfortable	favorite part of

Niagara Falls – An Amazing Trip

My brother and I ___like to travel___(1) by train. When you travel by train, ____________(2) everything around you. It's fast ____________(3), and you don't have to watch the roads or the other cars.

Last summer, ____________(4) to Niagara Falls, New York. We ____________(5) days. First, we went to the state park and walked on the trails. We stopped to see the falls and take some pictures. The falls are incredible!

The next day, we took a boat, the Maid of the Mist, to the falls. You should do it sometime. It was definitely my ____________(6) the trip. We really enjoyed the boat ride, but ____________(7): If you go on the Maid of the Mist, ____________(8) get wet! Also, ____________(9) a camera. You'll want to take a lot of pictures.

B Complete the sentences. Circle *a* or *b*.

1. The writer went to Niagara Falls by ____.
   a. car
   (b.) train
2. The writer traveled with ____.
   a. his cousin
   b. his brother
3. They walked on the ____.
   a. falls
   b. trails
4. The writer's favorite part of the trip was ____.
   a. the boat ride
   b. the train trip

LESSON 3 GRAMMAR

A Match the clauses to make sentences.

__c__ 1. When Ana looks at the engine,
____ 2. Before he started the car,
____ 3. He found the problem
____ 4. I asked about the engine
____ 5. Before we fix a problem,
____ 6. After they wash the car,

a. he fixed the rearview mirror.
b. they'll go to the gym.
c. she always checks the oil.
d. when he stopped the car.
e. when I took the car to the mechanic.
f. we read about it in the owner's manual.

B Put the events in each sentence in order. Write *1st* (first) or *2nd* (second). If the events happen at the same time, write *same.*

1. I called Sak before I went to class.

   ____1st____ ____2nd____

2. Before Dennis takes a long car trip, he checks everything on his car.

   ________ ________

3. Pat picked up her car after the mechanic called.

   ________ ________

4. I turn on the headlights when it is dark.

   ________ ________

5. We look at the tires before we get in the car.

   ________ ________

6. Trong looked at the directions after we got lost.

   ________ ________

C Read the sentences. Circle the correct words.

1. Nati will check the directions (before / after) she takes a trip.
2. She will have a mechanic look at the car (after / before) she leaves.
3. (When / Before) she is on the road, she'll stop every two hours for a break.
4. She always puts on her seat belt (after / when) she takes a trip.
5. Fatah and Rachid didn't check the gas tank (after / before) they went on their trip.

D Answer the questions with complete sentences. Use the words in parentheses.

1. When did you study? (before, come to class)

   I studied before I came to class.

2. When does Sao change the oil in his car? (before, take a trip)

   ____

3. When will Irina call? (after, pick up her car)

   ____

4. When do you hear the noise? (when, turn left)

   ____

5. When does Otto use the turn signal? (before, make a turn)

   ____

E Complete the paragraphs with the simple present, simple past, or future. Use the verbs in parentheses.

Brian started a car trip this morning, but things are not going well. When he got to his car, he ___saw___ (1) that his front tire __________ (2) flat. (see, be) Also, he didn't check the directions before he __________ (3) home. (leave) Now he's lost and his car has stopped. It doesn't start when he __________ (4) the ignition. (turn on) His gas tank is empty!

Brian got out of the car to make a phone call. He didn't close the door of the car when he __________ (5). (get out) Oh no! Brian will have more problems when that big car __________ (6) the door! (hit)

A **Complete the conversation. Use the words in the box.**

to my manager	How much	don't work	two-year warranty	my final offer
work something out	It's going for	doesn't either	~~It has only~~	

Car dealer: This is a fantastic car. (1) It has only 25,000 miles on it, and it has a (2) ______.

Daniel: It sure is nice. (3) ______ is it?

Car dealer: (4) ______ $9,500. It's a terrific price.

Daniel: $9,500! But the headlights (5) ______, and the radio (6) ______!

Car dealer: Uhhh... Let me talk (7) ______.

Daniel: Would you accept $7,000?

Car dealer: That's not possible for such a nice car, but I'm sure we can (8) ______. It also has a new tires and new paint too.

Daniel: That is attractive. How about $8,100? That's (9) ______. I can't go any higher.

Car dealer: You've got a deal.

B **Complete the sentences with *and, too, either,* or *but.***

1. The headlights work, ___but___ the turn signals don't.
2. The radio doesn't work, ______ the lights don't either.
3. I like the car, and my brother likes it ______.
4. The car has a radio, ______ it doesn't have a CD player.
5. The tires don't look good, and the windshield doesn't ______.
6. I can't drive yet, and my friend can't ______.
7. He likes road trips, ______ she doesn't.
8. My sister bought a new car, and her friend did ______.
9. The radio doesn't work, and the turn signals don't ______.
10. The windshield is broken, ______ the license plate is missing.

DO THE MATH Go to page 92.

LESSON 5 READING

A **Read the letters. What kind of advice does Chris give?**

Ask Chris, The Car Guy

Dear Chris,

I need to buy a used car, but I want to be sure I don't get a lemon. What should I do?

Needs Wheels

Dear Needs Wheels,

If you buy a used car from a dealer, the lemon laws will cover you in most states. But check the laws in your state because not all states have exactly the same laws. And have a mechanic check out any used car for problems before you buy. Good luck!

Chris

Dear Chris,

I bought a new car last year. But now, after 15,000 miles, it isn't working very well. I've taken it to the mechanic for the ignition, the headlights, and the tires. Every few weeks, it's something different. Do I have a lemon?

Worn Out and Tired

Dear Worn Out and Tired,

Maybe yes, maybe no. Has the mechanic fixed each of the different problems? If so, then you just have a car with a lot of different problems. Have you taken the car in for the same problem three or four times? If so, then you might have a lemon. Keep a record of each problem, the date, the repair cost, the mechanic or garage, and the work done. A repair log[1] can show you if your car is a lemon or not.

Chris

Dear Chris,

What should I look for when I take a car for a test drive?

Millie Shoemaker

Dear Millie,

Drive the car on local streets, on the highway, and in traffic. Are you comfortable in the car? Can you see all around? Is the car quiet or noisy? Check the warranty on the car, too. If it's a used car, check the repair and maintenance log. Every dealer and car is different. I hope you find a car that fits your needs.

Chris

[1] log: record

B **Mark the sentences *T* (true), *F* (false), or *NI* (no information).**

_F_ 1. Lemon laws protect all cars.

____ 2. Always ask a mechanic to check a used car.

____ 3. All states have the same laws about lemons.

____ 4. If a car has a lot of problems, it is a lemon.

____ 5. Chris is a mechanic.

____ 6. A repair and maintenance log records car problems and work done.

A Read the travel journal.

July 12

We are packed and ready to drive to Nashville, TN. Before we started packing, we took the car to the mechanic. We always take the car to our mechanic before we take a long car trip.

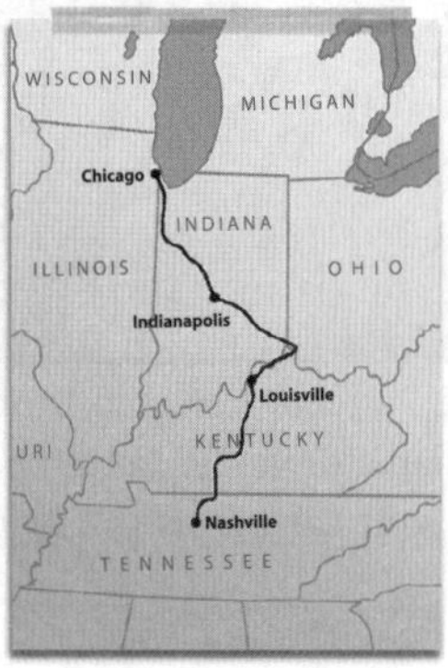

July 13

After we finished breakfast, we left Chicago. We drove south on Route 65 through Indiana. We stopped for lunch in Louisville, Kentucky. After lunch, we continued for about another four hours. Finally, we arrived in Nashville. When we got there, we found our motel and ate dinner. We went to bed early. We were really tired.

July 14

Nashville is not a large city, but there's a lot to do there. There are a lot of music stores and music museums. We took a bus tour of the city, and we went to the Country Music Hall of Fame too. We also saw the Grand Ole Opry[1] and walked around the stores. It was late so we didn't have time to go into many stores, and we didn't have time to buy any souvenirs either. After dinner, we went to a club to listen to some country music. Tomorrow, we'll visit Centennial Park before we go home.

[1] Grand Ole Opry: a famous country music concert hall

B Complete the tasks below.

1. Look at Joanie's journal for July 13. Find three sentences with a time clause in the simple past. Write them here.

   After we finished breakfast, we left Chicago.

   ____

   ____

2. Look at Joanie's journal for July 12. Find a sentence with a time clause in the simple present. Write it here.

   ____

3. Find a sentence with *but*. Write it here.

   ____

4. Look at Joanie's journal for July 14. Find a sentence with a time clause in the future. Write it here.

   ____

5. Find a sentence with *and...too*. Write it here.

   ____

6. Find a sentence with *and...either*. Write it here.

   ____

10 Crime Doesn't Pay

LESSON 1 VOCABULARY

A **Look at the pictures. Complete the safety flyer. Use the words in the box.**

walk alone	~~Lock the doors~~	commit a crime	Walk in
report it	arrest a suspect	Protect your wallet	

Keep Yourself Safe

At home:

- Lock the doors (1).
- Don't open the door if you don't know the person.

On the street:

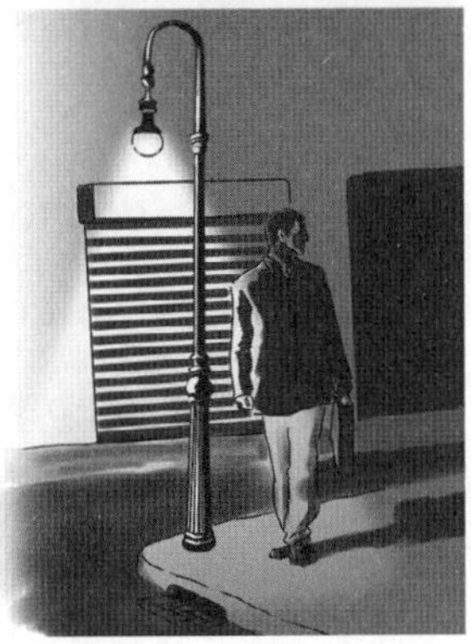

- Don't ______________ (2) at night.
- ______________ (3) well-lit areas.
- ______________ (4) or purse.

Remember, your help can make your neighborhood safe. If you see someone ______________ (5), let the police know. You must ______________ (6). Often, the police ______________ (7) because of help from the community.

B **Match the roles with the definitions.**

_e_ 1. The witnesses
____ 2. The defendant
____ 3. The attorney
____ 4. The jury
____ 5. The judge
____ 6. The courtroom

a. is the twelve people who decide the case.
b. is the person who listens to the case.
c. is the place where the trial is.
d. is the person on trial.
e. are the people who tell what they saw.
f. is the person who questions the witnesses.

A **Complete the article. Use the words in the box.**

to install a deadbolt lock	a peephole	~~home security~~
better lighting	sleep better	have a chain lock

Making Your Home a Safe Place

Have you ever thought about how to make your home a safer place to live? If you have, then you need to learn about ___home security___(1).

First, look at your home at night. Is it still dark in front of your house or apartment even when the lights are on? If it is, you may need to have ______________(2) at the front door.

Next, close the front door. Is there ______________(3) for you to look through before you open the door? How do you lock the front door? Do you ______________(4) for the door? That will keep you safe, but you might also want ______________(5). It's a very strong lock.

Talk to your neighbors about neighborhood security. If everyone works together, everyone will be safer, and you'll ______________(6) too.

B **Read the conversations. Circle the correct words.**

1. **A:** You should make your home safer.
   B: I know. I'll ((install better lighting) / sleep better) at my front door.
2. **A:** That's a good idea. What about your front door?
   B: I think I'll get a (peephole / deadbolt lock), so I can see who's there before I open the door.
3. **A:** You might also want to get a (better lighting / deadbolt lock) for the door.
   B: That's a good idea. I think I'll (sleep better / close the door) when I make these safety improvements.

A **Read the brochure. Underline seven sentences with gerunds as subjects.**

New Ideas from Code One

Code One's newest security system, Safety First, is making homes, offices, schools, and other buildings safer for everyone.

Keeping you safe is our most important job. Using our new system will make it more difficult for people to break in. People all around the state are protecting their homes and businesses with Safety First.

Entering a dark building at night doesn't have to be a problem. Using our lighting system is easy. With Safety First, people can turn on the lights before they enter. Our new system makes it easy to get help when you need it. Pushing just one button on your phone calls the police for you. Reporting a crime is faster than ever before.

Come and check out how Safety First home security system can help your family, friends, and co-workers be safe and happy! Staying safe is easy with Safety First.

B **Complete the sentences. Use the underlined verbs to make gerunds.**

1. Kara locks the windows every night.

   Locking______ the windows is the right thing to do.

2. She knows most of her neighbors.

   ____________ most of her neighbors is important.

3. She doesn't walk alone at night.

   ____________ alone at night can be dangerous.

4. She's going to install stronger locks on the door.

   ____________ stronger locks on the door is a good idea.

5. She doesn't carry a lot of money.

   ____________ a lot of money is not a good idea.

6. She never lets strangers in her house.

   ____________ strangers in your house isn't safe.

C **Read the sentences. Write *G* for gerund or *P* for present continuous.**

_P_ 1. The judge is listening to the questions and answers.

____ 2. Telling the truth is important in court.

____ 3. One witness is explaining what she saw.

____ 4. She's answering the attorney's questions.

____ 5. Making a decision is not always easy.

____ 6. The jury is thinking about what they heard.

D **Complete the sentences. Use a gerund or present continuous form.**

1. The people ___are watching___ their neighborhood. (watch)
2. ____________ lights is a good idea. (turn on)
3. Everyone ____________ sure their neighbors are safe. (make)
4. Right now, I ____________ a new lock. (install)
5. ____________ crimes can save lives. (report)
6. ____________ our neighborhood is everyone's job. (protect)

E **Look at the picture. What is Susan doing wrong? Complete the sentences with the present continuous or gerunds as subjects. Use the words in parentheses.**

1. (not turn on the lights)

   Susan ___isn't turning on the lights.___

   ___Not turning on___ the lights is a mistake.

2. (not lock the doors)

   Susan ____________.

   ____________ can be dangerous.

3. (not watch other people)

   Susan ____________.

   ____________ is a bad idea.

4. (not put down her coffee)

   Susan ____________.

   ____________ is a mistake.

Grammar note

Negative Gerunds

To form a negative gerund as subject, use *not* + gerund.

LESSON 4 EVERYDAY CONVERSATION

A **Complete the conversation. Use the words in the box.**

like to report	First, they broke	after that	what happened
suddenly ran	a complete report	Reporting this	~~How can I direct~~

Officer: Police Department. How can I direct (1) your call?

Witness: I'd ______ (2) a crime I witnessed.

Officer: Can you tell me ______ (3)?

Witness: Well, I was parking my car when I saw two men across the street. ______ (4) the window of Grant's Electronics. Then they took a TV.

Officer: What happened ______ (5)?

Witness: I think they saw me because they dropped the TV and ______ (6) away.

Officer: OK. Hold on, please. Another officer will fill out ______ (7). ______ (8) was the right thing to do.

B **Read the sentences. Circle the correct words.**

1. It's not safe to (leave / leaving) the windows open when you go out.
2. (Driving / Drive) alone at night can be dangerous.
3. It's a good idea to (lock / locking) the door when you get in the car.
4. It's good to (carry / carrying) a cell phone with you.
5. It's a mistake not to (turn / turning) on the lights when you get in the car.
6. (Walk / Walking) home alone at night is not a good idea.
7. (Install / Installing) good lighting outside the front door is a good idea.
8. It's smart to (protecting / protect) your wallet or purse.
9. It's a good idea to (talking / talk) to your neighbors.
10. (Listening / Listen) to good advice about safety is very important.

DO THE MATH Go to page 92.

A **Read the job ads. How much do these jobs pay?**

Help Wanted

Animal Control Worker
Salary: $33,450, full-time position.
Duties[1] include: picking up animals that are lost, sick, or dangerous; investigating[2] reports of animal abuse[3].
Qualifications[4]: high school diploma or GED; driver's license. Must enjoy working with animals.
Benefits: available for full-time employees. To apply: call 555-3211.

Fire Inspector
Salary: $53,700, full-time position.
Duties include: checking buildings for problems that can cause fires, investigating the causes of fires.
Qualifications: 5 years experience as a firefighter. College degree necessary. Must be able to solve problems.
Benefits: available for full-time employees. To apply: call 555-6789.

Driver's License Examiner
Salary: $25.00 per hour, part-time position.
Duties include: testing people's driving skills.
Qualifications: state driver's license and high school diploma.
To apply call: 555-0404

1 duties: what you do at work
2 investigating: finding more information about something
3 abuse: bad treatment
4 qualifications: the skills needed for a job

B **Read about the people. Answer the questions.**

1. Barbara has her driver's license. She's 21 years old, and she likes to work with animals. Which job should she apply for?

   ____

2. Reda has a college degree. He has worked as a firefighter for six years. Which job should he apply for?

   ____

3. Lena cannot work full time. She enjoys working with people. She is a great driver and has her high school diploma. Which job should she apply for?

   ____

A Look at the pictures. Read the script of a program.

Welcome to *Real-Life Crime* with Officer Bob. We start off tonight on a quiet evening. A woman is walking home from the bank. She's just cashed her paycheck. It's dark. Walking alone at night can be scary. It can also be dangerous. She hears a noise. Her hands are shaking as she opens her front door.

What can you do to make sure you don't become a crime victim? Following some simple safety rules can protect everyone from crime.

- It's a good idea to walk with a friend.
- It's important to find other people and a lighted area. Most criminals wait in dark places.
- It isn't safe to carry a lot of money with you.

We hope that you will think about what you have seen and heard on this program so you don't become a victim of a crime. Remember, watching the people around you can keep you safe.

B Look at A. Complete these tasks.

1. Find three sentences with gerunds as subjects. Write them here.

   Walking alone at night can be scary.
   ____
   ____

2. Find two sentences with the present continuous. Write them here.

   ____
   ____

3. Find four sentences with infinitives. Write them here.

   ____
   ____
   ____
   ____

That's Life

LESSON 1 VOCABULARY

A **Match the sentences with the life events.**

c 1. That's great! When will the wedding be?
____ 2. Congratulations! It's a boy!
____ 3. What are you planning to do now that you're finished with school?
____ 4. Congratulations! You started as assistant manager, and now you're the manager!
____ 5. I can't believe it! Now my daughter has a daughter.
____ 6. After 40 years at work, now you can relax!

a. get a promotion
b. retire
c. get engaged
d. become a grandparent
e. have a baby
f. graduate

B **Read the newspaper announcements. Complete the sentences. Use the words in the box.**

Birth	funeral	Death	~~Wedding~~	married	born

Johnsbury News **Section C**

Wedding (1) **ANNOUNCEMENTS**

Hannah and Peter Chavez

Hannah and Peter Chavez were ____________ (2) on July 20th. Both the bride and the groom graduated from Johnsbury High School last spring. The couple plans to live in Bradford.

____________ (3) **ANNOUNCEMENTS**

RICCIO – Sara Maria Riccio was ____________ (4) on July 29 to Blanca and Daniel Riccio.

____________ (5) **NOTICES**

Robert Howland

Robert Howland, age 95, died on August 10th. A ____________ (6) service is planned for August 14th at Wellwood Funeral Home.

A **Complete the requests. Use the words in the box.**

I'd like to suggest	~~reschedule our meeting~~	apologize for any inconveniences
take some of her shifts	fit into your schedule	Something's come up
Same time, same place	Please let me know	

John Feingold
To: Serena.diaz@cmail.com
Re: Need to Reschedule Meeting
Dear Ms. Diaz:

I am writing you to request that we reschedule our meeting (1) set for next Monday, November 3. A co-worker is on vacation, and I've been asked to ______ (2). ______ (3) that we meet the following Monday, November 10 at 10:30 in your office. Please let me know if this new meeting time will ______ (4). I ______ (5) this schedule change may cause.

Sincerely,
John Feingold
192 Commonwealth Ave.
Boston, MA 02116

John Feingold
To: Serena.diaz@cmail.com
Re: Need to Reschedule Meeting
Hey Serena - How RU?

I'm sorry but I need to change our meeting next Tuesday. ______ (6) and I can't make it. How about the following week? ______ (7)? ______ (8) if this works-thx!

L8R,
John

B **Read the invitation. Circle *a* or *b*.**

You Are Invited to a Graduation Party!
For: **Alex Savard** *Time:* **4 p.m. to 7 p.m.**
Date: **Saturday, June 15** *Place:* **542 Ridgewood Avenue**
RSVP: **555-8567**

1. The party is for ____.
   (a.) Alex
   b. Alex's family
2. The party is a celebration of a ____.
   a. wedding
   b. graduation
3. The party is on ____.
   a. Saturday, June 15
   b. 4 p.m.
4. The party is at ____.
   a. 542 Ridgewood Avenue
   b. Saturday, June 15

LESSON 3 GRAMMAR

A **Complete the sentences. Use the present passive and the verbs in parentheses.**

1. Every year, all our friends and relatives ___are invited___ to a party to celebrate my parents' anniversary. (invite)
2. Invitations ______________ by email. (send)
3. Our house ______________ by my brothers and sisters. (decorate)
4. The food ______________ by my aunts and uncles. (prepare)
5. The music ______________ by my brother's band. (perform)
6. Pictures ______________ by a friend. (take)

B **Write answers to the questions. Use the present passive and write complete sentences.**

Saturday Pool Parties at the Community Center This Summer!

Join us every Saturday from June to September!

Park opens:	10:00 a.m.	Dinner:	5:00 p.m.
Pool games:	2:00 p.m.	Movies:	7:00 p.m. to 8:30 p.m.
Pizza delivery:	4:45 p.m.	Pool closes:	9:00 p.m.

1. When is the park opened for the pool parties?
   It's opened at 10:00.
2. When are the pizzas delivered?
   ____
3. When is dinner served?
   ____
4. When are the movies shown?
   ____
5. When is the pool closed?
   ____

C Rewrite the sentences. Use the present passive with *by*.

1. Maggie picks the flowers for the weddings.
   The flowers are picked by Maggie.
2. Celia delivers the flowers.
   ____
3. A professional photographer takes the pictures.
   ____
4. The Jones Family Jazz Band performs the music.
   ____
5. Barry's Bake Shop bakes the wedding cakes.
   ____
6. The Green Meadows Restaurant prepares and serves the meals.
   ____

D Read the list. Then complete the paragraph with the present passive and *already* or *yet*.

Wedding "To Do" List

	Done	Not done
1. clean the house		✗
2. make the cake	✓	
3. decorate the backyard	✓	
4. wrap the gifts	✓	
5. wash the glasses		✗
6. prepare the food		✗

Grammar note

Already
Use *already* to talk about some time before now. *Already* comes before the past participle or at the end of the sentence.

Yet
Use *yet* to talk about some time up to now. With negative sentences, *yet* comes at the end of the sentence.

My sister's wedding is today! We've done a lot of things, but there is still so much to do before the wedding. I need to keep a list. The wedding will be at our house, but the house isn't cleaned yet (1). The cake ______________ (2). It looks great, and I hope it tastes good, too. The backyard ______________ (3). We did that last night. The gifts ______________ (4). We have enough plates and glasses, but the glasses ______________ (5). The food ______________ (6). My mother and aunts are in the kitchen cooking right now. I hope we finish everything by 2:00. That's when the wedding begins.

A Complete the conversation. Use the words in the box.

That's great	I'll be able to	~~got some good news~~
too bad	Let's celebrate	the bad

Todd: Hello, Fong? It's Todd. I've got some good news (1) and some bad news.

Fong: Oh, no. What's ______ (2) news?

Todd: Well, I took my GED today. It was really hard.

Fong: Oh, no. That's ______ (3).

Todd: Yes, but the good news is that I passed. Now ______ (4) apply for that manager's job at the restaurant.

Fong: Congratulations! ______ (5) news! ______ (6) tonight.

Todd: OK. I'll be home in a little while.

B Complete the sentences with *be able to* and the verbs in parentheses.

1. **A:** I hope you were able to go to the bank yesterday. (go)
   B: No, I wasn't. I ______ my paycheck. (not find)
2. **A:** Rick ______ to Maria's wedding next week. (not go)
   B: That's too bad. He ______ my graduation party last month either. (not attend)
3. **A:** Good luck on your test tonight. I'm sure you ______ easily. (pass) You studied very hard.
   B: Well, I ______ all the practice problems last night, so I'm a little worried. (not finish)
4. **A:** I ______ my aunt in the hospital this weekend. (visit)
   B: I'm so glad! I know you ______ last week. (not go)
5. **A:** She ______ him while he was in town. (not see)
   B: That's too bad. I know he ______ with her last time he was here either. (not meet)

DO THE MATH Go to page 93.

A **Read the brochure. Is it better to buy or to rent a home?**

To Buy or To Rent? That Is the Question

So you want to have your own home? Should you buy or rent?

If you buy,

you can make any changes you want to. You own it. It's yours. All the money you spend on your house goes to you.

But...

You are responsible for doing the repairs on the house. You may need to make a large down payment on your mortgage.[1]

If you rent,

you are not responsible for doing the repairs. Your security deposit[2] will be lower than the down payment[3] on a mortgage.

But...

You may have to ask the landlord if you can make changes. It doesn't belong to you. All the money you spend on rent goes to the landlord.

Here are some things you should think about before you rent or buy:

1. How much money can you pay each month?
2. What do you need and want in a home?
3. What kind of neighborhood do you want to live in?

Remember, your race, religion, familial status, or disability should not keep you from buying or renting a home. Everyone is protected by the Fair Housing Act.

[1]mortgage: the money you owe on your house
[2]security deposit: money you pay when you rent a house; you get the money back if you leave
[3]down payment: a first payment for something you buy

B **Mark the sentences *T* (true) or *F* (false.) If a sentence is false, rewrite it to make it true.**

_F_ 1. You are responsible for doing the repairs if you rent a home.

You are responsible for doing the repairs if you buy a home.

____ 2. You may need to make a large down payment on your mortgage when you buy a house.

____

____ 3. If you rent a house, you may have to ask the landlord if you can paint it.

____

____ 4. If you rent a house, it belongs to you.

____

____ 5. A security deposit is usually larger than a down payment on a mortgage.

____

A Read the list.

Dan and Linda's Wedding

	To Do	Who Will Do It
✔	print the invitations	
✔	arrange the flowers	
✔	bake the cake	
	take photos	Tran
✔	make the dress	
✔	set the tables	
	serve the food	the waiters
	make the coffee	Gourmet Catering
✔	decorate reception hall	
	greet the guests	Dan and Linda's family

B Look at the list in A. Write sentences about the things that are checked. Use the present passive.

1. The invitations are printed.
2. ______________________________
3. ______________________________
4. ______________________________
5. ______________________________
6. ______________________________

C Look at the list in A. Write sentences about the things that are not checked off. Use *will be able to* and the information in the chart.

1. Tran will be able to take the photos.
2. ______________________________
3. ______________________________
4. ______________________________

UNIT 12

Doing the Right Thing

LESSON 1 VOCABULARY

A **Match the pictures with the words.**

1
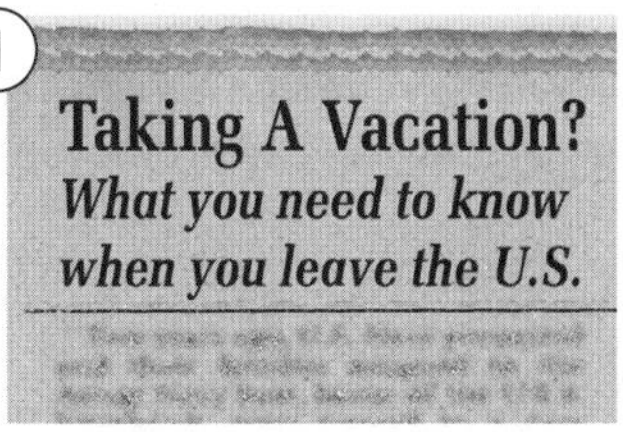
Taking A Vacation?
What you need to know when you leave the U.S.

2

NEW JURY IN KAPLAN COURT CASE

3

State Representative Speaks: Says He's Angry About New Law

4

Vote Now! It's Important!

5

Newspaper Doesn't Print the Real Story?

6

HUNDREDS OF PEOPLE MEET IN CITY PARK FOR PEACE MARCH

____ the right to a fair trial

__1__ the right to carry a U.S. passport

____ freedom of speech

____ freedom of the press

____ the right to vote

____ freedom of assembly

B **Match the questions with the answers.**

__c__ 1. Why should I obey the laws?

____ 2. Why should I pay taxes?

____ 3. How often do you have to serve on a jury?

____ 4. Why is it so important to be informed before you vote?

____ 5. What's the advantage of being a citizen?

____ 6. Whose rights should you respect?

a. You get full protection and rights guaranteed by the Constitution.

b. You should know what the political and social issues are.

c. If there were no rules, no one would be safe.

d. You should respect the rights of everyone equally.

e. It can be every year, but it's usually not that often.

f. The government uses the money to help everyone.

A Complete the letter. Use the words in the box.

to vote for the	It's very important to	volunteered at
work together to help	can make positive changes	~~get involved in~~

Subject: Letter to the Editor
From: Nancy Lozada
To: the Editor

Dear Editor,

I think it's important for people to ___get involved in___ (1) the community. In our neighborhood, we have a group called Neighbors Helping Neighbors. It's a group of people who ____________ (2) each other. I've ____________ (3) Deed's Elementary School. I've really enjoyed helping some of the kids.

There are other ways to help, too. My neighbor has a sign in his yard telling people ____________ (4) new senior center. In the past, he has spent a lot of time helping some of the seniors get to the clinic for appointments and to the store to do their shopping. ____________ (5) help each other. Together, we ____________ (6) in our community.

Nancy Lozada

Libertyville, Illinois

B Mark the sentences *T* (true), *F* (false), or *NI* (no information).

__T__ 1. Neighbors Helping Neighbors is a volunteer group.

____ 2. Nancy volunteers at the elementary school.

____ 3. Nancy wants to be a teacher.

____ 4. There's going to be a vote about a new senior center.

____ 5. Her neighbor puts signs in his yard about voting.

____ 6. He drives seniors to the movies.

A **Read the schedule. Complete the sentences with infinitives.**

Danville Community Festival

Time	Activity	Volunteers to work
10:00–2:00	sell tickets	Malik
11:00	start race	Mark
11:00–1:00	run	Jim, Renee
12:00–2:00	serve food	Pavel, Ines
2:00	announce winner	Mark
4:00–5:00	clean up	all

1. Malik volunteered ___to sell___ tickets at 10:00.
2. At 11:00, Mark is planning ______________ the race.
3. Jim and Renee decided ______________ in the race from 11:00 to 1:00.
4. Pavel and Ines agreed ______________ food for two hours.
5. At 2:00, Mark needs ______________ the winner of the race.
6. From 4:00 to 5:00, all the volunteers are planning ______________.

B **Answer the questions. Use the words in parentheses.**

1. **A:** What does Betsy want to do tomorrow? (go to the mall)
   B: ___She wants to go to the mall.___
2. **A:** What does she plan to do there? (buy new shoes)
   B: ______________
3. **A:** What do you need to do? (study for my math test)
   B: ______________
4. **A:** What did they decide to do? (stay home)
   B: ______________
5. **A:** What did Daniel agree to do for the Community Festival? (sell tickets)
   B: ______________
6. **A:** What did Elizabeth volunteer to do? (prepare sandwiches)
   B: ______________

C Read the sentences. Circle the correct gerund or infinitive.

1. I don't enjoy (meeting / to meet) new people.
2. We didn't practice (playing / to play) the music before the meeting.
3. Dan doesn't plan (volunteering / to volunteer) next week.
4. He decided (working / to work) instead.
5. Manuela really dislikes (cleaning / to clean) up.
6. She hopes (helping / to help) another time.

D Can the sentence be rewritten as verb + infinitive? If it can, rewrite the sentence. If it can't, write *NCP* (no change possible).

1. I'll begin studying at 8:00. I'll begin to study at 8:00.
2. We enjoy reading the newspaper. ______
3. Our neighbors like talking to us. ______
4. My cousin dislikes doing his homework. ______
5. He likes playing basketball. ______
6. We'll continue working on this tomorrow. ______

E Read the chart. Write sentences about the people.

	Like	Dislike	Hope
Ed	travel	study	visit Australia
Marie	read	exercise	get a job in a library
Greg and Julie	play sports	cook	start a neighborhood volunteer group

1. Ed likes traveling. (or Ed likes to travel.)
He dislikes studying.
He hopes to visit Australia.
2. ______
______
______
3. ______
______
______

A Complete the conversation. Use the words in the box.

he do that	any idea why	can I help you	don't know what
I've lived	I think I can	think it's because	~~told me to come in~~

Omar: Hello. I called yesterday. The man on the phone told me to come in (1).

Ms. Davies: How ____________ (2) today?

Omar: Well, I ____________ (3) to do. ____________ (4) in the same apartment for ten years. Two weeks ago, the new landlord told us to move. Now I don't have a place to live.

Ms. Davies: Do you have ____________ (5)?

Omar: No. I pay my rent and follow the rules. I ____________ (6) he wants to give the apartment to someone else. Can ____________ (7)?

Ms. Davies: No, he can't. ____________ (8) help you.

B Read about Omar. Then write the reported requests.

Yesterday Omar talked to Ms. Davies about a problem with his landlord. Ms. Davies told him to do some things.

1. Ms. Davies said, "Fill out this form."
   Ms. Davies told Omar to fill out this form.
2. Ms. Davies said, "Answer these questions."
   ____
3. Ms. Davies said, "Don't use a pencil."
   ____
4. Ms. Davies said, "Write down your information."
   ____
5. Ms. Davies said, "Continue to be a good tenant."
   ____

DO THE MATH Go to page 94.

A **Read the article. What important events happened in Alabama?**

Civil Rights in Alabama

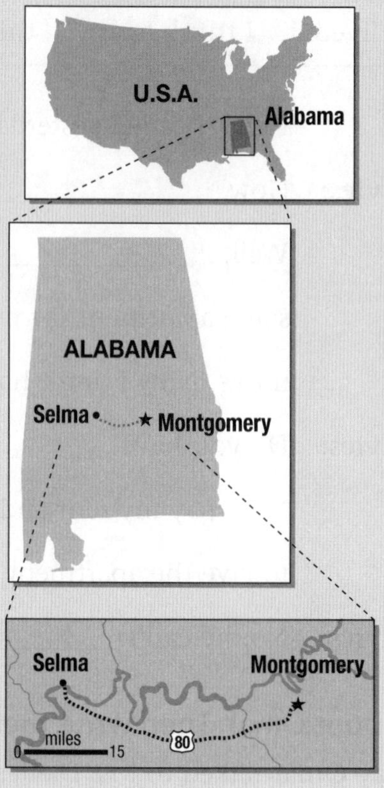

March 7, 1965
Many African Americans were not allowed to vote. Six hundred people started marching out of Selma, Alabama, to protest this discrimination[1]. The marchers traveled only six blocks before they were beaten back[2] by state and local police. Many marchers were hurt in this push for civil rights.

March 9, 1965
Martin Luther King, Jr. led a second march to the Pettus Bridge to protest the beatings on March 7.

March 15, 1965
After hearing the reports of the violence in Alabama, U.S. President Lyndon B. Johnson signed the Voting Rights Act. This promised the right to vote to all American citizens.

March 21, 1965
After receiving court protection, 3,200 marchers began a third march from Selma to the state capitol in Montgomery.

March 25, 1965
After five days of marching (12 miles per day) and sleeping in fields, 25,000 marchers arrived in Montgomery.

August 15, 1965
Congress passed the Voting Rights Act.

[1] discrimination: different treatment because of sex, race, or religion
[2] beaten back: fought against and forced to stop

B **Write answers to the questions. Use complete sentences.**

1. Where did the marches begin on March 7, 1965?

   The marches began in Selma, Alabama.

2. Who was the leader of the march to Pettus Bridge?

   ____

3. Who was the president of the U.S. in March 1965?

   ____

4. What city did the people march to?

   ____

5. How many people arrived there?

   ____

6. What law was passed by Congress because of the marches?

   ____

Write sentences and questions. Use the words in the boxes.

I	like	live	to	the city
you	enjoy	volunteer	in	the hospital
she/he	plan	go	at	the park
they		play		the school
		exercise		the senior center
				the health center
				Florida

Sentences

1. I enjoy volunteering at the senior center.
2. ____________________
3. ____________________
4. ____________________
5. ____________________

Questions

1. Did they plan to go to Florida?
2. ____________________
3. ____________________
4. ____________________
5. ____________________

DO THE MATH

UNIT 1

Read the information. Find the percentages for what the people said. Then label the charts with the correct percentages.

1. A survey asked 800 students about their career plans. Here's what they said.

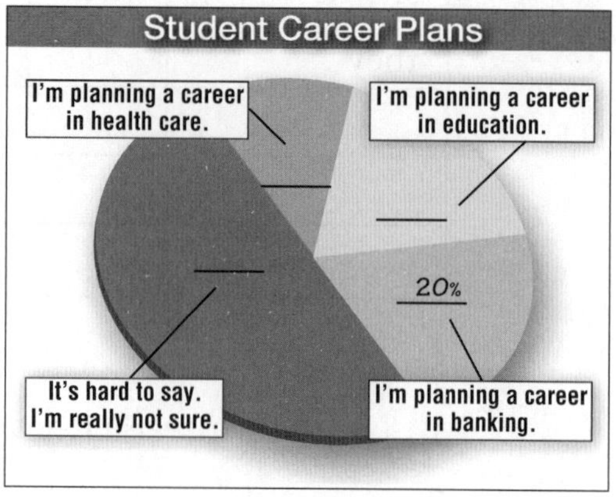

160 students: "I'm planning a career in banking."

a. 160 ÷ 800 = .2 or 20%

144 students: "I'm planning a career in education."

b. ______________________________

96 students: "I'm planning a career in health care."

c. ______________________________

400 students: "It's hard to say. I'm really not sure."

d. ______________________________

2. A survey asked 8,000 workers about their careers. Here's what they said.

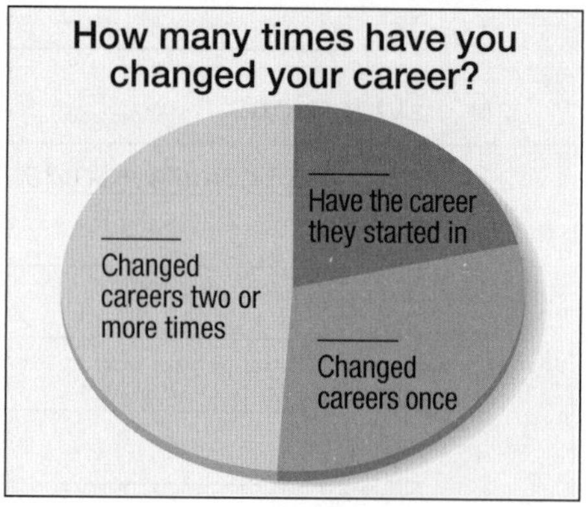

1,680 workers: "I have the career I started in."

a. ______________________________

2,400 workers: "I changed careers once."

b. ______________________________

3,920 workers: "I changed careers two or more times."

c. ______________________________

UNIT 2

A **Read the paragraph and the information in the ad. Then answer the questions.**

Sharon and Mike are going to the baseball game at the stadium. Sharon is bringing her three younger cousins. One cousin is 15 years old. One cousin is 11 years old. Her youngest cousin is five years old. Sharon gives the man at the ticket counter $50 for the tickets for everyone.

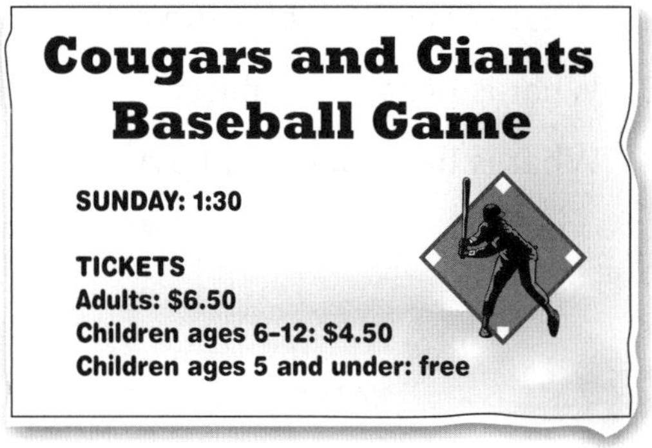

1. What is the total cost of the tickets? __________
2. How much change will Sharon receive? __________

B **Read the paragraph and the information on the sign. Then answer the questions.**

The Adams family is going to the *Taste of Greenville* festival at the stadium. Mr. and Mrs. Adams have a teenage daughter, a seven-year-old son, and a four-year-old daughter. Mrs. Adams gives the woman at the ticket counter $40.00 for tickets for all the family members.

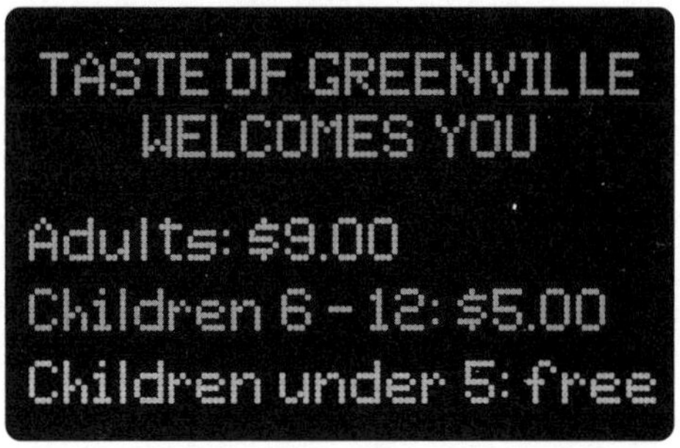

1. What is the total cost of the tickets? __________
2. How much change will Mrs. Adams receive? __________

UNIT 3

Read the information in the charts. Then answer the questions.

1. What is Maddie's best subject? __________
2. What is her worst subject? __________
3. What is her grade point average? __________

Name: Maddie Hanel Grade: 11

English	B	(3.0)
History	C	(2.0)
Math	A	(4.0)
Science	B	(3.0)
Art	B	(3.0)

4. What is Jonathan's best subject? __________
5. What is his worst subject? __________
6. What is his grade point average? __________

Name: Jonathan Drew Grade: 10

English	B+	(3.5)
Math	B+	(3.5)
History	B+	(3.5)
Science	A	(4.0)
Art	B	(3.0)

UNIT 4

Read the information in the paragraphs. Then answer the questions.

1. The Grand Hotel manager has offered a promotion to Sokanna. The job is Wednesday through Sunday from 2:30 p.m. to 10:30 p.m. The pay will be $21.50 per hour.
   a. How much is the gross pay for each day Sokanna works? __________
   b. How much is the gross pay per week? __________
2. The Springfield General Hospital manager has offered Miguel a job. The hours for the job are Tuesday through Saturday from 8:30 to 3:30. The pay will be $23.50 per hour. Miguel currently makes $770 gross pay per week at his current job.
   a. How much is the gross pay per week for the new job? __________
   b. Will Miguel make more or less money at Springfield General Hospital? __________

UNIT 5

A Read the information in the graph. Then complete the sentences.

1. About 25 percent of the people in Windsor volunteered in __________.
2. Volunteering did not increase between __________ and __________.
3. Between 1990 and 2015, volunteering increased by about __________ percent.

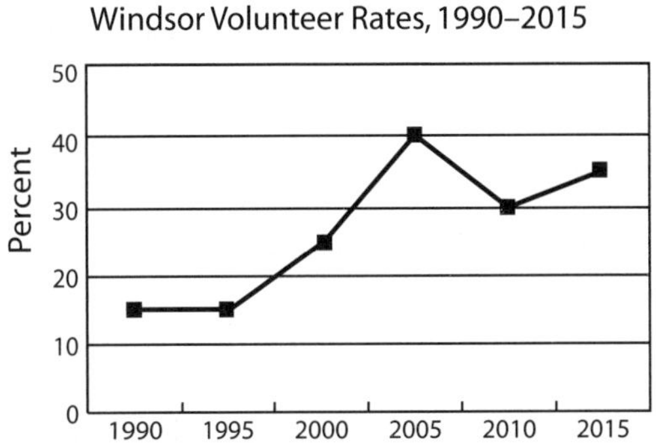

B Read the information in the chart. Then answer the questions.

1. What percent* of people in Minneapolis volunteered? __________
2. What percent* of people in San Francisco volunteered? __________
3. What percent* of people in Washington, D.C. volunteered? __________
4. Which city has the highest percent of volunteers? __________

	Population	Volunteers
Minneapolis	3,300,000	1,221,000
San Francisco	7,150,000	2,109,000
Washington, D.C.	6,100,000	2,013,000

**Round to the nearest percent.*

UNIT 6

Read the information in the bills. Then answer the questions.

1. How much money should you leave for a 15% tip* at Mario's Pizzeria? __________
2. If you leave a 15% tip*, how much will you pay for the food, tax, and tip? __________

Check "Mario's Pizzeria"		
2	slices of pizza @ 3.75 each =	$7.50
1	soup @ 2.50 each =	$2.50
1	tea @ 1.50 each =	$1.50
1	lemonade @ 1.15 each =	$1.15
	SUB TOTAL:	$12.65
	Tax @ 8%:	$1.01
	TOTAL:	$13.66

3. If you leave a 15% tip*, how much will you pay for the food, tax, and tip at Bob's Burger Barn? __________
4. How much more will you pay if you leave a 20% tip*? __________

**Calculate a tip using the SUB TOTAL. Round to the nearest cent.*

Check "Bob's Burger Barn"		
3	hamburgers @ $6.00 each =	$18.00
2	turkey burgers @ $5.50 each =	$11.00
3	lemonades @ $2.00 each =	$6.00
1	coffee @ $1.50 each =	$1.50
	SUB TOTAL:	$36.50
	Tax @ 8%:	$2.92
	TOTAL:	$39.42

UNIT 7

A Read the information. Then answer the questions.

1. Greg has $3,000 in a savings account. He receives 4% interest on this account. How much interest will he earn this year?

   $3,000 × .04 = __________

2. Ana receives 5% interest on her savings account. How much interest will she earn this year on $2,500?

   $2,500 × .05 = __________

B Read the information in the chart. Then answer the questions.

1. Sara wants to open a savings account with $500. Which account can she get?

   ____

2. Adam has $10,000 in a Premiere Savings account. How much interest will he earn this year?

   $10,000 × .05 = __________

Town Bank Savings Accounts
Compare our accounts.

	Interest rate	Minimum balance
Basic Savings Click to Apply	2%	None
Gold Savings Click to Apply	4.03%	$2,500
Premiere Savings Click to Apply	5%	$8,000

UNIT 8

Read the information in the paragraphs and the charts. Then answer the questions.

1. Sara had a busy weekend. On Saturday morning, she took care of her friend's children for two hours. In the afternoon, she went on a 90-minute bike ride. On Sunday, Sara went to the gym. She went swimming for one hour and lifted weights for 30 minutes.

Activity	Calories/hour
swimming	320
bike riding	350
taking care of children	200
lifting weights	180

   a. How many calories did Sara burn on Saturday? __________

   b. How many calories did she burn on Sunday? __________

   c. Did Sara burn more calories on Saturday or Sunday? __________

   d. Which activity burns the most calories per hour? __________

2. Mario had a busy weekend too. On Saturday, he played soccer for three hours. After that, he came home and vacuumed his apartment for 30 minutes. Then he played the guitar for an hour. On Sunday, he went for a one-hour bike ride. Then he played soccer again for 90 minutes.

Activity	Calories/hour
bike riding	350
playing guitar	175
playing soccer	400
vacuuming	200

   a. How many calories did Mario burn on Saturday? __________

   b. How many calories did he burn on Sunday? __________

   c. On which day did Mario burn more calories? __________

   d. Which activity burns the most calories per hour? __________

UNIT 9

Read the problems. Then answer the questions.

1. Amarjit drives 15,000 miles per year. His car gets 30 miles per gallon. The average price of gas last year was $2.10 per gallon. How much did Amarjit spend on gas last year*? __________
2. Lilia also drives 15,000 miles per year. Her car gets 34 miles per gallon. The average price of gas last year was $2.10 per gallon. How much did Lilia spend on gas last year*? __________
3. Who spent more money on gas: Amarjit or Lilia? __________
4. Josh gets his car's oil changed every three months. The price of an oil change is $45.99, but every fourth one is free. How much did he pay for oil changes last year*? __________

**Round to the nearest cent.*

UNIT 10

Read the information in the graphs. Then answer the questions.

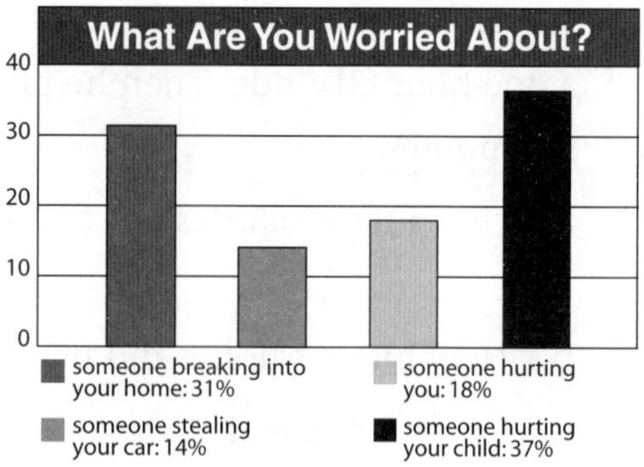

1. A survey asked 1,000 people what crimes they were most worried about.
   a. What crime are people most worried about?

   ____

   b. What crime are people least worried about?

   ____

   c. How many people are worried about someone breaking into their home?

   ____

Source: Loveland, Colorado Police Department

2. A second survey asked 200 people what crimes they were most worried about.
   a. What crime are people most worried about?

   ____

   b. What crime are people least worried about?

   ____

   c. How many people in the survey were worried about school safety?

   ____

UNIT 11

A Read the information. Then answer the questions.

1. Mei and Jack are planning a retirement party for their father. Look at their budget and plans. How many people will they be able to invite to the party?

   ____

2. If they want to invite 10 more people, how much will the party cost?

   ____

Retirement Party for Dad

Budget:	$2,000
Room:	$225
Band:	$275
Dinner:	$15 per person, including the tip

B Read the information. Then answer the questions.

1. Leon and Yuan are planning their wedding reception. The band will cost $400. The reception hall will cost $300 to rent. Dinner will cost $25 per person, including the tip. Leon and Yuan plan to spend $3,200 for their reception. How many people will they be able to invite?

   ____

2. After the wedding, Leon and Yuan want to go to San Francisco for three nights and four days for their honeymoon. The plane tickets are $300 each and the hotel is $175 a night. They plan to spend $150 a day on food and entertainment. How much will the trip cost?

   ____

Read the information in the voter polls. Then answer the questions.

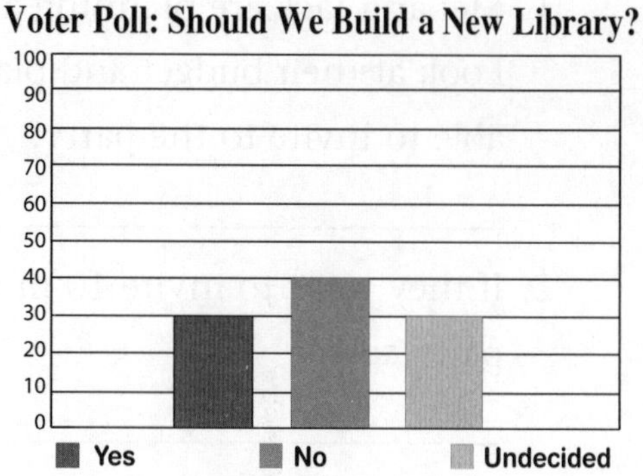

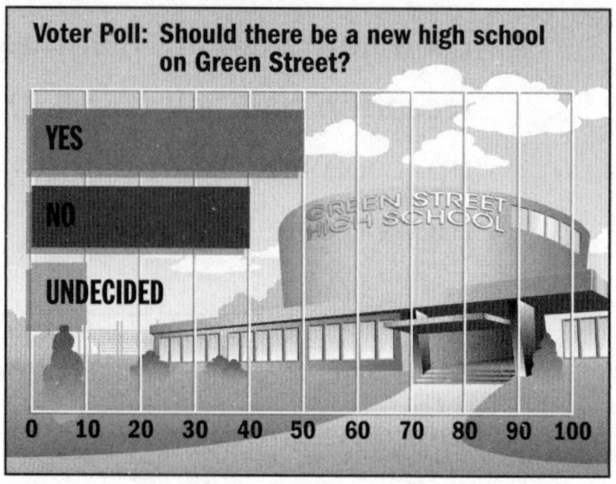

1. Do most people want a new library?

____

2. If half of the undecided people vote *yes* for the library, will the library be built?

____

3. How many undecided people must vote *yes* for the library for it to pass?

____

4. How do most people feel about the high school?

____

5. If half of the undecided people vote *no* for the high school, which side will win?

____

6. How many undecided people must vote *yes* for the high school to pass?

____